LB
3060.3
.H37
2002

GRIDGE

GARFIELD RIDGE BRANCH

T3-BNO-066

What Every Parent Needs to Know about Standardized Tests

CHICAGO PUBLIC LIBRARY
GARFIELD RIDGE BRANCH
6348 ARCHER AVE.   60638

What Every Parent Needs to Know about Standardized Tests

How to Understand the Tests and Help Your Kids Score High!

Joseph R. Harris, Ph.D.

McGraw-Hill
New York   Chicago   San Francisco
Lisbon   London   Madrid   Mexico City
Milan   New Delhi   San Juan   Seoul
Singapore   Sydney   Toronto

McGraw-Hill

A Division of The **McGraw·Hill** *Companies*

Copyright © 2002 by Joseph R. Harris. All rights reserved. Printed in the United States of America. Except as permitted under the United States Copyright Act of 1976, no part of this publication may be reproduced or distributed in any form or by any means, or stored in a database or retrieval system, without the prior written permission of the publisher.

1 2 3 4 5 6 7 8 9 0   FGR / FGR   0 9 8 7 6 5 4 3 2 1

ISBN 0-07-137758-1

This book was set in Garamond Book by Inkwell Publishing Services. Printed and bound by Quebecor World/Fairfield Graphics.

McGraw-Hill books are available at special quantity discounts to use as premiums and sales promotions, or for use in corporate training programs. For more information, please write to the Director of Special Sales, Professional Publishing, McGraw-Hill, Two Penn Plaza, New York, NY 10121-2298. Or contact your local bookstore.

 This book is printed on recycled, acid-free paper containing a minimum of 50% recycled, de-inked fiber.

CHICAGO PUBLIC LIBRARY
GARFIELD RIDGE BRANCH
6348 ARCHER AVE.   60638

R02066   81856

Dedication

To my son, Ross Adam Harris, who sometimes goes by the Tsalagi (Cherokee) name Guwisgui. I am so proud of the person you are. If I could have written down a wish list with everything my child would be, I couldn't be more pleased. Not only are you the most intelligent person I have ever met, but you have the kindest heart. I can't wait to see what your future holds for you.

CONTENTS

Acknowledgments

I can't imagine completing a work such as this without being indebted to a large group of friends, family, and professionals who have contributed their time, information, love, support, resources, and patience. Where to begin? I owe so many people so much.

I must thank Ellen Haley, vice president of CTB/McGraw-Hill, for her help not only on this book but on my previous McGraw-Hill books as well. She never hesitated to give me permission to reprint the TerraNova reports that helped me explain what test scores mean. I also wish to thank my agent, Bert Holtje, for taking on this neophyte to non-academic publishing and being in my corner. Thanks also to Barbara Gilson of McGraw-Hill, who was also my executive editor on the *Get Ready! for Standardized Tests* series, and whose vision guided this book. Thanks too to Jennifer Chong, editorial assistant at McGraw-Hill, who has been a tremendous resource and has never hesitated to help with this book, as she did with the *Get Ready! for Standardized Tests* series. And who can forget Jane Palmieri, editing manager, McGraw-Hill, who has kept my nose to the grindstone through the editorial process.

I can't end this acknowledgment without thanking my wife, Elaine, for her patience and encouragement through yet another writing project. She has made my writing projects possible by her support and indulgence. Whenever I was discouraged, she urged me to continue. And my son, Ross Adam Harris: I don't recall a time when I didn't see myself through his eyes. He is the brightest light in my universe.

Last but not least, I owe more thanks than I can ever express to my friend, my writing mentor, my e-mail buddy, my greatest cheerleader and most demanding task mistress, Carol Turkington. She is everything a great teacher should be.

Introduction

Remember the standardized tests we took in school? The tests were long and boring, and by the time we finished with them, we were worn out. Those tests are still around. Every school year, many of our children take them, and every year local newspapers and television news programs devote tremendous amounts of coverage to their results. Today, the stakes for students are different from what they were in the past, but they are just as serious as they were back then.

Technically, a standardized test is any measure used to evaluate skills or characteristics, with specific procedures for administering and scoring the tests and interpreting the results. This book will discuss the type of standardized tests known as group achievement and aptitude tests that schools administer to students.

Testing History

Standardized testing has its roots in the industrialization of America at the turn of the nineteenth century, when rural

Americans left the farms in droves to seek work in city factories. This new wave of workers created a need for literate employees who could read instructions, write reports, and perform basic mathematical functions.

At the same time, government began to increase support for public education. Blue-collar workers began sending their children to school so they could train for better jobs.

During this period, psychologists Alfred Binet and Theodore Simon in Paris developed the forerunner of today's intelligence test to help identify children likely to have trouble in school—but their test was given to each child individually and was therefore quite expensive.

As World War I funneled recruits from all educational backgrounds into the military, commanders needed quick ways to determine which soldiers were capable of learning particular skills. Searching for a way to evaluate recruits in a fast and cost-effective manner, two group tests of ability were developed for the Army—these tests were the forerunners of today's group standardized tests used in schools.

After the war was over, psychologists and educators began to realize the benefits that standardized tests might bring to the nation's schools. In 1923, the Stanford Achievement Test became the first group achievement test used in the schools. This test, currently in its ninth revision, continues to be one of the most popular group achievement tests today.

Group standardized achievement testing caught on, and in the 1920s and 1930s became the darling of American public education. Psychologists placed great faith in the value of such tests to diagnose a student's learning abilities. In fact, by the 1930s, psychologists believed that the group standardized achievement tests available at that time were superior to individually administered tests because of their objectivity, ease of scoring, and standardized conditions. They looked forward to a time when schools would test first graders to help plan the type of instruction most suited to them. They envisioned testing all children every year not only to determine how successfully they were learning but also to figure out which teaching strategies worked the best.

Educators eagerly embraced these tests because they thought the tests offered an objective and accurate way of determining a student's needs. Group standardized tests allowed educators to evaluate many children at a small cost per child—certainly at a cost much lower than for individual testing.

Unfortunately, group standardized tests never lived up to their early promise. Researchers discovered that the very characteristics that make standardized tests so efficient and cost-effective also limit their validity in evaluating the learning of individual students.

By the 1960s and 1970s, after decades of ability grouping based on standardized tests, it became clear that such practices were not acceptable. Parents sued school districts for placing their children in rigid educational "tracks" based on test scores. Parents and civil rights groups won a series of landmark court cases challenging ability grouping (or tracking), and the courts told the schools that they could no longer place children into different instructional groups on the basis of group standardized test results. Researchers also began to identify racial and gender biases in group standardized tests.

The Accountability Movement

Just as the courts began to restrict the use of standardized tests for ability grouping, taxpayers began to demand of their schools more accountability. By the early 1980s, voters began to demand evidence that schools were spending their tax money responsibly.

Parents became suspicious of the ways educators gauged how effectively they taught students. The public became suspicious of any but the most objective measures of student performance. To parents, group standardized tests seemed to be the ideal tool to gauge academic progress.

Politicians began to promise to boost the amount of testing and the consequences of test scores for students, teachers, and educational systems themselves. Today many states use standardized tests in "high-stakes testing" as the basis for:

- Promotion and retention
- Graduation
- Eligibility for remedial programs
- Eligibility for gifted programs
- Teacher evaluations, including firing teachers whose students consistently perform poorly on standardized tests
- Evaluations of administrators, firing administrators in schools and school districts in which students consistently perform below national standards
- School district funding

Along with the increasing importance of standardized test scores, there have been testing scandals. Teachers have been fired or prosecuted for stealing copies of standardized tests and drilling their students on the correct answers as a way of boosting test scores used to evaluate teaching skills. Some school districts have been accused of unethical practices such as:

- Creating "flu lists" of students who consistently perform poorly on standardized tests and are told to stay home during test week

- Intentionally classifying underperforming students as being eligible for special education classes to exclude them from taking standardized tests
- Teaching only items included on standardized tests and neglecting important subject matter that the tests don't cover

Two Types of Standardized Tests

The two main types of group standardized tests that your child may take in public school are: *norm-referenced tests* and *criterion-referenced tests.* Let's take a look at each of these.

Norm-Referenced Tests

The main distinguishing feature of norm-referenced tests is that students' scores are judged by comparing them with the scores of a sample of students who took the test during standardization.

For example, let's say that in Test A, the *average* score for norm-group students was 200. If your child scored 227, this means she scored above the average level, but we don't know how much above average she scored. If you look at the statistics of the scores from the norm group, this reveals that 57 percent of norm-group students scored at or below a score of 227. That provides you with a much better idea of exactly how your child's score measures up. Chapter 3 provides a more extensive discussion of what norm-referenced scores mean. The major commercial tests are norm-referenced.

Criterion-Referenced Tests

In criterion-referenced tests, students are compared against some criterion for success. For example, when your child was learning to tie his shoes, you engaged in simple criterion-referenced testing: In this case, your criterion for success was that your child tied a square knot in bows, and the knot held for some period of time. It didn't matter what score he got compared with those of others—just that he met the criterion. If your child couldn't tie his shoes, there would be a hierarchy of skills that lead up to the final goal of tying the proper knot, such as knowing how to loop the shoelaces, how to tighten the laces, how to tie a square knot. If your child demonstrated that he could loop and tighten the laces but couldn't tie a square knot, the next order of business was to teach him to tie a square knot.

Schools give criterion-referenced tests to determine what specific skills students have mastered and what they have not. For example, Elaine takes a criterion-referenced test in mathematics. She meets the criteria for mastery in counting to 20, adding single-digit numbers without carrying, and subtracting single digits not requiring borrowing. She doesn't meet criteria for mastery of any higher mathematics skills that come next, such as adding and subtracting single-digit numbers with regrouping, adding and subtracting two- and three-digit numbers, and so on.

Her teacher would see that Elaine doesn't need further work to teach her addition and subtraction of single digits without carrying and borrowing and that she can proceed to the next skills on the list. In this example, it doesn't matter how Elaine compares with other students. Her teacher is only concerned with the specific skills Elaine has mastered.

Most criterion-referenced tests used by states are non-commercial tests that the states have developed themselves.

State-by-State Breakdown
of Standardized Tests

Tables I-1 and I-2 provide information about standardized tests on a state-by-state basis. Table I-1 lists which standardized tests public schools use in each state use, and Table I-2 specifies which grades the schools test as well as whether students must pass a test to receive their high school diplomas.

Note that more than half the states conduct some type of group standardized testing, and many require students to pass an "exit exam" to receive their high school diplomas. Even if you live in a state that doesn't require standardized tests, your child may still participate in some type of standardized testing through local testing programs. Also note that these data frequently change.

Table I-I Norm-Referenced and Criterion-Referenced Tests Administered by State

STATE	NORM-REFERENCED TEST	CRITERION-REFERENCED TEST	EXIT EXAM
Alabama	Stanford Achievement Test		Alabama High School Graduation Exam
Alaska	California Achievement Test	Alaska Benchmark Examinations	
Arizona	Stanford Achievement Test	Arizona's Instrument to Measure Standards (AIMS)	
Arkansas	Stanford Achievement Test		
California	Stanford Achievement Test	Standardized Testing and Reporting Supplement	High School Exit Exam (HSEE)
Colorado	(None)	Colorado Student Assessment Program	
Connecticut		Connecticut Mastery Test	
Delaware	Stanford Achievement Test	Delaware Student Testing Program	
District of Columbia	Stanford Achievement Test		

STATE	NORM-REFERENCED TEST	CRITERION-REFERENCED TEST	EXIT EXAM
Florida	(Locally Selected)	Florida Comprehensive Assessment Test (FCAT)	High School Competency Test (HSCT)
Georgia	Stanford Achievement Test	Georgia Kindergarten Assessment Program—Revised and Criterion-Referenced Competency Tests (CRCT)	Georgia High School Graduation Tests
Hawaii	Stanford Achievement Test	Credit by Examination	Hawaii State Test of Essential Competencies
Idaho	Iowa Tests of Basic Skills/Tests of Achievement and Proficiency	Direct Writing/Mathematics Assessment, Idaho Reading Indicator	
Illinois		Illinois Standards Achievement Tests	Prairie State Achievement Examination
Indiana		Indiana Statewide Testing for Educational Progress	
Iowa	(None)		
Kansas		(State-Developed Tests)	
Kentucky	Comprehensive Test of Basic Skills	Kentucky Core Content Tests	

STATE	NORM-REFERENCED TEST	CRITERION-REFERENCED TEST	EXIT EXAM
Louisiana	Iowa Tests of Basic Skills	Louisiana Educational Assessment Program	Graduate Exit Exam
Maine		Maine Educational Assessment	High School Assessment Test
Maryland		Maryland School Performance Assessment Program, Maryland Functional Testing Program	
Massachusetts		Massachusetts Comprehensive Assessment System	
Michigan		Michigan Educational Assessment Program	High School Test
Minnesota		Basic Standards Test	Profile of Learning
Mississippi	Comprehensive Test of Basic Skills	Subject Area Testing Program	Functional Literacy Examination
Missouri		Missouri Mastery and Achievement Test	
Montana	Iowa Tests of Basic Skills		

STATE	NORM-REFERENCED TEST	CRITERION-REFERENCED TEST	EXIT EXAM
Nebraska	(None)		
Nevada	TerraNova		Nevada High School Proficiency Examination
New Hampshire		NH Educational Improvement and Assessment Program	
New Jersey		Elementary School Proficiency Test/Early Warning Test	High School Proficiency Test
New Mexico	TerraNova		New Mexico High School Competency Exam
New York		Pupil Evaluation Program/Preliminary Competency Tests	Regents Competency Tests
North Carolina	Iowa Tests of Basic Skills	NC End of Grade Test	
North Dakota	TerraNova	ND Reading, Writing, Speaking, Listening, Math Test	
Ohio		Ohio Proficiency Tests	Ohio Proficiency Tests
Oklahoma	Iowa Tests of Basic Skills	Oklahoma Criterion-Referenced Tests	

STATE	NORM-REFERENCED TEST	CRITERION-REFERENCED TEST	EXIT EXAM
Oregon		Oregon Statewide Assessment	
Pennsylvania		Pennsylvania System of School Assessment	
Rhode Island	Metropolitan Achievement Test	New Standards English Language Arts Reference Exam, New Standards Mathematics Reference Exam, Rhode Island Writing Assessment, and Rhode Island Health Education Assessment	
South Carolina	TerraNova	Palmetto Achievement Challenge Tests	High School Exit Exam
South Dakota	Stanford Achievement Test		
Tennessee	Tennessee Comprehensive Assessment Program	Tennessee Comprehensive Assessment Program	
Texas		Texas Assessment of Academic Skills, End-of-Course Examinations	Texas Assessment of Academic Skills
Utah	Stanford Achievement Test	Core Curriculum Testing	

STATE	NORM-REFERENCED TEST	CRITERION-REFERENCED TEST	EXIT EXAM
Vermont		New Standards Reference Exams	
Virginia	Stanford Achievement Test	Virginia Standards of Learning	Virginia Standards of Learning
Washington	Iowa Tests of Basic Skills	Washington Assessment of Student Learning	Washington Assessment of Student Learning
West Virginia	Stanford Achievement Test		
Wisconsin	TerraNova	Wisconsin Knowledge and Concepts Examinations	
Wyoming	TerraNova	Wyoming Comprehensive Assessment System	Wyoming Comprehensive Assessment System

13

STATE	KG	1	2	3	4	5	6	7	8	9	10	11	12	COMMENT
Kansas				X		X	X	X	X	X	X	X		
Kentucky					X	X	X	X	X	X	X	X	X	
Louisiana				X	X	X	X	X	X	X	X	X	X	
Maine					X				X			X		
Maryland				X		X	X	X	X	X	X	X	X	
Massachusetts				X	X	X		X		X	X			
Michigan					X	X		X	X					
Minnesota				X		X	X	X	X	X	X	X	X	
Mississippi				X	X	X	X	X	X					
Missouri			X	X	X	X	X	X		X	X			

STATE	KG	1	2	3	4	5	6	7	8	9	10	11	12	COMMENT
Montana					X				X			X		The State Board of Education has decided to use a single norm-referenced test statewide beginning in the 2000–2001 school year.
Nebraska	**	**	**	**	**	**	**	**	**	**	**	**	**	**Decisions regarding testing are left to the individual school districts.
Nevada					X				X					Districts choose whether and how to test with norm-referenced tests.
New Hampshire				X			X				X			
New Jersey				X	X			X	X	X		X		
New Mexico					X		X		X					
New York				X	X	X		X	X	X			X	Assessment program is going through major revisions.
North Carolina	X			X	X	X	X	X	X	X			X	NRT Testing selects samples of students, not all.

STATE	KG	1	2	3	4	5	6	7	8	9	10	11	12	COMMENT
North Dakota					X		X			X		X			
Ohio					X		X				X				
Oklahoma				X		X		X	X			X		
Oregon				X		X			X		X			
Pennsylvania						X	X		X	X		X		
Rhode Island				X	X	X	X	X	X	X	X			
South Carolina				X	X	X	X	X	X	X	X	***	***	***Students who fail the High School Exit Exam have opportunities to take the exam again in Grades 11 and 12.
South Dakota		X			X	X			X	X		X		
Tennessee		X		X	X	X	X	X	X						

STATE	KG	1	2	3	4	5	6	7	8	9	10	11	12	COMMENT
Texas				X	X	X	X	X	X	X	X	X	X	
Utah	X	X	X	X	X	X	X	X	X	X	X	X	X	
Vermont					X	X	X		X		X	X		Rated by the Centers for Fair and Open Testing as a nearly model system for assessment.
Virginia				X	X	X	X		X	X	X	X		
Washington					X			X			X			
West Virginia				X	X	X	X	X	X	X	X	X		
Wisconsin					X				X		X			
Wyoming					X				X			X		

19

The "Big Four"

If your state requires standardized testing, your child will almost certainly take tests from one of four commercially available testing packages:

- TerraNova (which includes one version featuring the Comprehensive Tests of Basic Skills and the other featuring the California Achievement Test)
- Iowa Tests of Basic Skills
- Metropolitan Achievement Test
- Stanford Achievement Test

This book will discuss each of these tests and how to interpret their scores, and it will also review aptitude testing.

Help Your Child Succeed

M ost of us remember the days when we took group standardized tests in school. We moved into and out of reading groups and were placed into high, middle, or low sections of our classes mainly based on our teacher's judgment. We walked across the stage and received our high school diplomas if we earned passing grades in the required subjects, and no one asked us whether we had passed an exit test.

It's a different world today. Many school districts and states today use standardized tests to determine what level of classes children should attend, what classes are open to them, and even whether they may graduate. Government officials have recommended expanding standardized testing to all school districts, with stricter consequences for low student scores.

Tricks and Gimmicks

For years, rumors of various "tricks" and techniques that supposedly give students an advantage in answering questions when they don't know the answers have floated about. Some authors came up with statistical analyses of past standardized tests and advised students that when in doubt, they should never answer D, for example.

In the past, some of those techniques were valid. Some test producers unintentionally constructed tests in such a way that they created predictable answer patterns. Test producers today are on the lookout for test response patterns and take steps to avoid them. The strategies of yesterday just don't work anymore.

How to Raise Test Scores

There are only two legitimate ways to help students score as high as possible on group standardized tests:

1. Help your child become as strong as possible in the academic areas the tests evaluate.
2. Eliminate any factors that hamper your child's performance.

Making students academically stronger is something you should strive for every day. Since the tests are supposed to assess a very broad curriculum, it makes sense that you can best raise your children's test scores by helping them learn as much as possible.

But removing factors that interfere with your child's test performance is something most parents don't think about. In the following sections, we'll explore ways of accomplishing both.

Before the Test

You may hear experts recommending that you change your child's diet, bedtime, and exercise routine before he or she takes a standardized test—but that's a mistake. Instead, decide that you want to help your child be better prepared in mind and body to do well in *school,* not just on standardized tests. Look at your child's lifestyle and try to identify areas that you need to change to make him or her a better student in general, and make any changes as soon as possible.

Sleep Well

The vast majority of children and adolescents are sleep-deprived, according to research. Many children stay up late surfing the Internet, stay late at school for lessons or activities, or stay up late to watch a favorite TV show. Sleep deprivation can take its toll, and you will see some pretty dramatic effects of even small amounts of sleep loss that is spread out over weeks and months. Children with even minor sleep deprivation have trouble paying attention, remembering what they have read, making good decisions, and understanding new concepts.

However, don't wait until the night before the test to send your child to bed early. Instead, make any changes in bedtime gradually—weeks before the test. If your fourth grader is staying up past 11 p.m. each night and you want to shoot for a 9:30 p.m. bedtime, start by having him go to bed at 10:30 p.m. this week, then 10 p.m. next week, and then 9:30 p.m. the following week.

You may have to make the change even more gradually—perhaps in 15-minute increments, week by week. The point is that you want to make sure you don't present a disruption the night before the test.

Eat Right

Is your child a picky eater? As you ferry your child from school to soccer practice to oboe lessons, you both probably grab a handful of whatever is quick and convenient. Medical studies are revealing that even many young children have the beginnings of coronary artery disease.

Our eating habits are making us fat, but they are also interfering with our attention, our memory, and our comprehension. Children with poor eating habits perform more poorly in school, and hence more poorly on standardized tests.

Take a look at your child's dietary habits and see what you need to change—then make the change weeks before important events such as standardized tests. If your child is used to eating a piece of toast and slugging down a soft drink in the car on the way to school, suddenly presenting him with a good breakfast on the morning of the test will disrupt his ability to do well.

If he's not accustomed to eating a lot of protein in the morning, a high-protein breakfast will make him sleepy and may give him a stomachache. If he's accustomed to sugary cereal or a toaster pastry and you give him whole-grain cereal with wheat germ and yogurt on the side, he might have trouble digesting it all.

Identify the best eating habits for an efficient learner and implement as many changes as you can weeks in advance. Good nutrition is beyond the scope of this book, so we'll leave it to you to identify a good, healthy diet for your family. But be aware that proper nutrition can greatly increase your child's ability to learn, and poor nutrition can cripple that ability.

Be Fit

It's a sad fact: Many of our children today are becoming couch potatoes. Unfortunately, in many parts of the country physical education classes are either few or nonexistent in the elementary grades. Even in middle and high school, students only take physical education for part of the year, and once they have satisfied their P.E. requirement, never take it again.

Dr. Kenneth Cooper, the former Air Force cardiologist who popularized aerobics exercise programs, has documented the benefits of aerobic fitness, including mental clarity, increased ability to focus attention, and the physical endurance to work for long periods of time. Dr. Cooper and others have demonstrated time and again that people who are physically fit learn better, retain information longer, and are happier about learning than their nonfit peers. Students who are aerobically fit say they are just plain better students.

Look at your child's exercise habits. Is she getting at least 40 minutes of sustained physical activity four to six times a week? If not, look into available programs. Community and local organizations sponsor sports teams, karate classes, bicycle clubs, skate parties, and all sorts of other activities for your child. Talk to an exercise trainer, your pediatrician, or your child's physical education teacher. Find a program for your child and encourage her to put down the video game controller, get off the couch, and get physical.

Does your daughter enjoy ice skating? Many ice-skating rinks offer skating lessons and have skating leagues. Does your son enjoy watching hockey on TV? Find an age-appropriate hockey league.

The point here is to get your child's heart pumping and blood flowing. It doesn't have to be organized sports, and it doesn't matter what *type* of exercise—just make sure your child enjoys doing it so he or she will continue.

Emotions

As important as it is to do well on standardized tests, keep in mind that your child is still a child, with a child's emotions and need to feel good about himself. He still has a child's need for play. Remember that all work and no play makes Jack a disgruntled student who has trouble paying attention and who won't do as well on tests as he could if he had a little joy in his life.

If your child has adopted an all-work-and-no-play lifestyle, encourage her to do something that gives her pleasure each day. Happy children do better in school and love learning.

Make sure that your child doesn't suffer from test anxiety. Most students feel some degree of apprehension, which is normal. However, a few rare students become so paralyzed with fear when confronted with a test that they can't perform. Impress on your child that the tests are important, but don't let her see you wringing your hands over them, and don't desperately badger her about doing her best.

If your child tells you he's worried about the tests, or if you see signs of anxiety, reassure your child as best you can. Point out how hard he's been working in school. If he's doing well in school, chances are he'll do well on the standardized tests, too.

If your child stops eating, lies awake at night worrying about the tests, or seems to be depressed about doing poorly, you need to get some professional help. Talk to her pediatrician, who can discuss appropriate treatments. If outside counseling seems appropriate, your child's pediatrician will know which professionals in your town are trained to counsel children. Or look in the Yellow Pages for psychologists and psychiatrists who specialize in working with children's anxiety.

Answer Sheet Savvy

Your child may not have any worries about the tests, but can he fill in the answer sheets correctly? Sometimes the optical scanning equipment can't accurately determine children's answers. Perhaps your child has too many erasures on her answer sheet. Or maybe her attempt to fill in a bubble on the sheet was too sloppy. You may want to practice bubbling in answers with your child. Use the practice sheet in Figure 1-1 to determine whether your child can fill in the bubbles appropriately.

Figure 1-1   Bubbling-In Practice Sheet

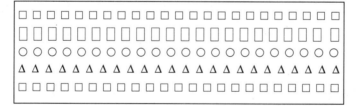

The practice sheet includes most of the shapes that children would normally encounter on test optical scanning sheets. Have your child practice both filling in and erasing marks on the practice sheet to make sure that she fills in the shapes completely and that she erases completely.

Ideally, your first concern should be to help your child become as strong as possible academically instead of worrying about how well he performs on standardized tests. But if you want to get a sense of the areas in which your child will be tested, Chapters 8 through 12 discuss major commercial tests your child might encounter and describe the broad academic areas that each test assesses. You also can look over the parent information booklet that some schools send home before testing. Such booklets generally provide information on what areas the tests will evaluate.

Identify Weak Skills

Most parents know if their child is a poor reader or really strong in math. Look over your child's report cards. Is there a particular subject area that consistently needs work? Look for any teacher comments. Notes such as "Jimmy just doesn't seem to understand multiplication," or "Janie reads words well, but she has problems with understanding what she reads," can alert you to weak areas.

Talk to your child. Do any of his subjects frustrate him? Many children are astute judges of their own strengths and weaknesses and can give you valuable insights.

Talk to your child's teacher. If you're worried about specific grades or you notice that your child consistently struggles with homework in the same subjects, the teacher can tell you whether or not others in the class are having similar problems. Maybe the school has adopted a new math curriculum that everyone is struggling with. Or maybe the school district has implemented stricter grading guidelines so that last year's "above average" is this year's "average." Perhaps your child is in an honors class in which an "average" is equal to an "excellent" in regular courses. Your child's teacher can also discuss what you can do at home to reinforce what your child does at school.

Look over your child's past standardized test results. (If you can't find them, the guidance counselor will have copies.) Skip ahead to Chapter 3 and use the guidelines given in the chapter to interpret the scores and identify your child's strengths and weaknesses. Do you see particular patterns? These past reports can help you identify areas on which he might score lower on upcoming tests.

Study Skills

One of the best ways for your child to become a better student is to take advantage of what teachers are trying to teach. That sounds pretty obvious, but if children don't have the skills to understand, organize, and study the material they're given, it doesn't matter how good the instructional program or how competent the teacher.

As you help your child with her homework, assess her study skills. How does she approach homework? Is she sloppy and disorganized? Does she often forget to bring home the right textbook? Maybe she can only complete assignments when someone is standing over her and telling her what to do.

Make sure your child understands how to organize schoolwork. Does his teacher require color-coded file folders or a different spiral-bound notebook for each subject? Maybe your child is supposed to use one giant three-ring binder with divider tabs separating the subjects.

If you have younger children, you may have to organize the materials for them at first. As you proceed, involve them in the organization and discuss why you are putting the papers where you're putting them. You may have to go through your children's backpacks every day after school and show them where to put all the stray papers, worksheets, and handouts. Then repeat the procedure after homework is finished by placing homework papers where they should go. Even many older students don't know how to organize their materials and can benefit from some help.

Preparing for Classroom Tests

Does your child know how to review the homework once she has organized it? Many children don't realize that one reason they organize their materials is to help them review for classroom tests. Show your child how to check the homework assignment, worksheets, and handouts to get an idea what the teacher thinks is important and to prepare for tests. Often, making a grand outline, concept map, or topic list of the concepts covered will help your child understand the logical organization of the material.

Taking Notes

Most teachers don't expect children to be able to take notes in elementary school, but they do expect them to begin to be learning to take notes by middle school.

To many students, note taking is a difficult skill, especially if they were never taught how to take notes. Many students have trouble summarizing, and they try to write down every word the teacher says. Others don't take any notes because they aren't sure what's important. Ask your child's teacher if note taking is something your child should be doing.

Reading

A problem in reading can hold your child back in more than just language arts. Does your child read well? How is her vocabulary? Does she understand what she reads? Even if you receive precious little information on how well your child is doing in other subjects, you are likely to receive detailed feedback on how well she reads. If your child has a problem reading, ask her teacher what you can do at home to help and whether your child needs a tutor.

Reading to your child is one of the best ways to prepare him for a lifetime of learning. Most of us read to our children when they are small, but even children beyond third or fourth grade still enjoy being read to. Your child probably has favorite books he wants you to read over and over, but find other books on a wide range of topics and read them as well. Find out what interests your child. When you go to the library or the bookstore, have him help you pick out books he will be interested in having you read to him.

As your child gets older, have him participate in reading. You read a paragraph and then have your child read the next one. Eventually, he can take over most of the reading, and you can be there to define words he doesn't know. Encourage your child to read a wide range of books, magazines, and newsletters.

If your child enjoys the Internet, find some sites that cater especially to children (such as www.familyplanet.com), where your child can find age-appropriate stories, news for children, and fun activities. For some reason, many children are much more motivated to read material online than they are in their books.

Visit the library regularly, and make sure your child has his own library card. Some libraries issue children library cards as soon as they are old enough to ask for them; others have age restrictions. When you go to the library, make sure your child knows where to find books appropriate for his age.

Classroom Skills

Make sure your child has strong classroom skills. One of the most important classroom skills is listening. Walk down the hallways of any school at any grade level and peep into the classrooms. You'll see some students looking around or playing, and a few will even have their heads down on the desk. No wonder that when their parents ask them what they learned at school that day, they say, "Nothing."

It doesn't matter how good the curriculum is if your child doesn't listen. Look at comments on her report card: Do several teachers make note that she's not a good listener? If your child has serious problems listening, you need to rule out hearing problems and attention deficit disorder. Most children receive hearing screenings when they begin school. If it's been some time since your child had a hearing test, ask for one. If your child seems to have a hearing problem, school personnel or your pediatrician can refer you for further diagnostic evaluations.

If you think your child has attention deficit disorder, discuss your concerns with both your child's teacher and his pediatrician. If inattentiveness is causing major disruptions in your child's life, it may be necessary to have both his pediatrician and a qualified psychologist perform diagnostic tests.

In many cases, you'll find that your child is not listening well in school because he has never learned how to listen. Listening is like any other skill—you must learn how to do it well. It may help to practice listening skills, especially with younger children.

While you read to your young child, stop from time to time and ask her to repeat the story. It's not necessary for her to repeat the story word for word; paraphrasing the story accurately in her own words is a more productive skill. Play car games such as "I'm going to repeat 10 words, and I want to see who can remember the most." While your child is watching a favorite TV program, ask her from time to time to tell you what she heard.

Another important classroom skill is asking questions. Many students miss out on valuable information in school because they are afraid or reluctant to ask questions. Make sure your child knows that most teachers welcome questions. Questions show that students are interested in what they are learning and care enough to make sure they understand it. Tell the teacher if your child is afraid to ask questions.

On Test Day

Test Morning

Do what you can to help your child minimize conflict on the morning of the test. Don't choose that morning to take away your teenager's car keys because his interim grade report is dismal, or to ground him for breaking curfew last week. If he has been having conflicts with another child on the bus, drive him to school.

Do what you can to help your child be as relaxed as possible on the morning of the test. Encourage her to dress comfortably in her favorite clothes and comfortable shoes. Make sure she has readied the necessary clothes and supplies the evening before so that she doesn't have to rush the next morning.

If your child seems nervous on the morning of the test, don't brush aside his fears. Listen to his feelings. Encourage him to remember how well he's doing in school; don't dwell on his anxieties. After you have listened to his concerns and made attempts to reassure him and divert his attention, move on. Hand him his lunch, wish him a good day, and say good-bye.

There are some other things that you can do on the morning of the test that will help your child. Make sure she wears her watch so she can keep track of how much longer she has on the test.

Have your child take a handkerchief or tissues. If he develops a runny nose and must get up and run to the teacher's desk to get tissues, that will disrupt his progress through the test and take time away from reading and answering questions.

Have her take extra, sharpened pencils. Having to get up continually to sharpen pencils will take time away from the test and disrupt her flow of thoughts.

During the Test

This section contains advice for your child. Depending on his age, you might read over this section and then teach these points to your child—or have him read this section for himself.

Following Directions

Make sure your child understands the importance of following test directions. It's crucial that she listen to the teacher's directions so that she knows what she is supposed to do.

It's also necessary with some students to make sure they take the tests seriously. School administrators frequently report that students either leave their test papers blank or use the bubbles to make pictures. Some have produced beautiful pictures of horses, houses, and people by selectively filling in bubbles. But, of course, their answers meant nothing. Teachers report that some students sit with their heads down and don't respond to the tests at all. Make sure that your child understands that the tests are important and that he must make every effort to do his best.

Test Questions

Your child should read the entire question before answering. Many students hastily answer questions and miss vital information about what the questions are really asking. If the question is a multiple choice, your child should read all the possible answers before choosing one—there may be clues within the body of the question or in the answers that can point to the correct answer. Students should be wary of absolutes such as *always* and *never.*

If your child isn't sure about an answer and test instructions allow her to mark in her test booklet, she should flag the question and return to it later. She should answer questions she knows first and then use any time left over to return to the questions she has flagged.

A related strategy to the one above is useful with multiple-choice test questions. If your child is confronted with a multiple-choice question and can't choose the correct answer, suggest that he cross out the answers that he knows are incorrect. That way he will be faced with choosing from fewer options without distraction by the answers he knows are wrong.

If a student thinks that she should change an answer, she should do so. Research has shown that students more often change their answers from incorrect ones to correct ones than from correct ones to incorrect ones. But your child should make sure that she completely erases the original answer mark on the answer sheet, or the computer won't be able to discriminate which answer was intended.

Your child should be on guard for distractors—pieces of information in the question or the answer alternatives that draw the student's attention away from what is really important. For example, consider the following test question:

---

1   The bus stopped once on Wildmere Way, twice on Camelot Drive, and twice on Reidville Road. The driver's name was Gus, and Gus was 49 years old. How many times did the bus stop?

[Answer: 5]

The sentence "The driver's name was Gus, and Gus was 49 years old" is a distractor: It isn't relevant to solving the problem. After reading the questions, the astute test taker will ignore that sentence and focus instead on the first sentence, which tells him that the bus stopped five times.

One useful strategy students can use in determining whether an answer is correct is to simply ask themselves, "Does it look right?" or "Does it sound right?" This strategy can be particularly useful when the student is stumped.

Accompanying artwork usually provides useful information that can suggest the correct answer. Many students rush through questions and try to answer them without paying attention to artwork. Test publishers don't put the art in there for no reason.

For example, on a standardized test asking questions about distance, there might be a map of two towns—Greer and Bellville, with Maplewood in between. On the map, it appears that Maplewood is about a third of the distance from Bellville than Greer is. Consider the following multiple-choice question:

---

1 Greer and Bellville are 21 miles apart on Highway 290. T. J. drove 30 miles an hour from Greer to Bellville. He reached the town of Maplewood in 27 minutes. How long should it take him to go from Maplewood to Bellville?

A 28 minutes

B 15 minutes

C 60 minutes

D 5 minutes

Students who are strong in math could figure out this problem just by the way the question is worded. But the student who's not so good in math could look at the map and see that Maplewood is about twice as far from Greer as it is from Bellville, so it should be half as far from Maplewood to Bellville as it is from Greer to Maplewood, or about $13\frac{1}{2}$ minutes. Since answer B, 15 minutes, is the closest to $13\frac{1}{2}$ minutes, the astute student can reasonably conclude that B is the correct answer.

2

Scoping Out Test Questions

We've all had experience in taking standardized tests, but have you ever wondered just who it is who's responsible for coming up with those questions? Constructing questions for standardized tests is both a science and an art.

In regard to the science of constructing a test, researchers have discovered how students approach test questions, what elements of the questions encourage them to respond in certain ways, and what elements make it more likely that students' answers will accurately reflect what they know.

Basically, test makers want to find out what students know. To do this, they use advanced statistical methods to construct test questions that are technically sound. Each year, after thousands of students have taken the tests, the test makers get to work analyzing the results to learn which questions help them accurately determine what students know. They also develop ways to help identify answer sheets on which students have marked their answers in a random manner.

But there is an art to constructing test questions as well. Realizing that many students find standardized tests boring and don't try to do well, test makers try to get as creative as they can to develop interesting questions and graphs, charts, and pictures.

Types of Test Questions

Whether it's in the classroom or on a standardized form, testing relies on two primary types of questions: recognition questions and recall questions.

Recognition

Because standardized test questions must be written so that computers can score them, recognition questions are usually the questions of choice. Recognition questions can be constructed so that students can answer them simply, by coloring in bubbles on answer sheets.

Typically on standardized tests, the test taker must recognize the correct answer from a group of alternatives, all but one of which is incorrect. Although it would be possible to simply offer a series of true/false questions, standardized achievement tests generally avoid them. Rather, they employ multiple-choice questions, usually with four or five alternatives labeled A through D or E. For example:

---

1   What is George Washington's nickname?
    A King of the Gypsies
    B Father of Our Country
    C Great Emancipator
    D Clown Prince of Baseball

A child's success with such questions only depends on the ability to recognize the correct answer among a group of incorrect ones.

There are several important elements of multiple-choice questions: stems, options, and distractors.

Stems.   The text of the question is the stem. "What is George Washington's nickname?" is a stem. In longer questions, the stem may include multiple sentences, requiring the child to sift through large amounts of information to determine what is relevant to answering the question. For example, the stem may be something such as:

---

2   Carol went to visit her grandmother, who lives in Springfield. She and her daughter Kara first took a taxi to the train station, and then they took the train from Greely to Johnson City. From there, they took a commuter flight to Harleyville. They rented a car in Harleyville and drove to Carol's grandmother's house in Springfield, which is 60 miles from the airport.

There is a lot of information in the sample question above. If we are asking what relation is Kara to Carol's grandmother, your child must be able to figure out that all the information about transportation and the distance from Springfield to the airport is irrelevant to answering the question, and that the only pertinent information is that (1) they are visiting Carol's grandmother and (2) Kara is Carol's daughter. However, if the question asks how many different types of transportation Carol and Kara took, the information about whom they are visiting and how far Springfield is from the airport is irrelevant.

Many children have problems with stems because they don't read all the information, or they read it and don't separate the relevant from the irrelevant. Imagine Bill's consternation when he selects D as the correct answer to the following question:

---

3   Martin Luther King, Jr., was never
    A President of the United States.
    B a resident of Atlanta, Georgia.
    C a father.
    D a minister.

[Answer: A]

Bill may know full well that Dr. King was a minister, but perhaps he rushes through the question and does not notice the word never. Many children rush through and answer questions without understanding or paying attention to all the information the stems contain.

Options.   These are the answer alternatives from which the student gets to choose. Some alternatives are straightforward and require the child to choose the correct answer from among different alternatives. For example:

---

4 George Washington was the first

 A person to walk on the moon.

 B author to write a novel in the English language.

 C President of the United States.

 D husband of actress Julia Roberts.

[Answer: C]

Other questions may offer options that are very similar. For example:

---

5 Before becoming President in 1992, William Jefferson Clinton was the

 A U.S. Senator from Arkansas.

 B U.S. Representative from Arkansas.

 C Governor of Arkansas.

 D Chief Justice of the Arkansas State Supreme Court.

[Answer: C]

In the above example, most students are likely to know that former President Clinton is from Arkansas and served in some elected office in that state, but they may not recall exactly what office. In this example, the child must demonstrate a more exact knowledge of the President's background than if the options presented more dissimilar choices such as:

A Governor of Arkansas

B quarterback of the Carolina Panthers

C star of the TV show *Frasier*

D lead guitarist for The Stray Cats

Distractors. Distractors are options that confuse or mislead those who are unsure about their answers. They can help separate out those who actually have a strong knowledge of the subject from those who have a shaky knowledge. For example:

---

6   Sir Arthur Conan Doyle was the
    A Prime Minister of England.
    B first husband of Princess Anne of England.
    C actress Catherine Zeta-Jones' husband.
    D author of the Sherlock Holmes books.

[Answer: D]

The person who is not very familiar with the name Sir Arthur Conan Doyle will see the title "Sir" and the British-sounding name and surmise that this person probably has some connection with Great Britain. All the options could be plausible answers to someone who is unsure of the correct answer.

The wise student will know how to deal with distractors by eliminating the impossible answers first. If permitted, he will cross out the impossible answers on the test booklet to narrow down the options.

In the above example, perhaps the older child knows that Michael Douglas is Catherine Zeta-Jones' husband and crosses out that option, narrowing the options to three instead of four. Now the student would have a one in three chance of choosing the correct answer rather than one in four. If he could eliminate one more answer as being impossible, he could narrow the odds to one in two.

Recall

The second type of question, recall, consists of two main types of questions: short-answer and essay questions. Both types require a deeper understanding of subject matter than do recognition questions and, in many cases, an even deeper understanding that allows the test taker to synthesize the information and make informed judgments.

Short-Answer Questions. These questions require that the test taker provide brief answers, ranging from single words to only a sentence or two—for example, "Who delivered the Gettysburg Address?" Short-answer questions can be very effective teaching tools. Such questions encourage students to dig deeper into their understanding of the material.

Essay Questions. From the standpoint of testing depth of learning, essay questions are at the top of the heap. They require the test taker not only to have a thorough understanding of the subject but to be able to apply and organize the information. An essay question might ask: "In two pages or less, describe the major conflicts, besides slavery, that led to the Civil War." Or perhaps the question will ask the test taker to demonstrate the ability to analyze complex information, such as "Was the practice of affirmative action fair? Justify your answer, for or against, using the United States Constitution."

Of course, the major disadvantage of short-answer and essay questions is that they can't be scored by machines. At present, it's impossible to provide short answers on optical scanning sheets.

Answers to essay questions pose even greater obstacles, because the scoring is highly subjective. How can someone objectively score an essay about a favorite memory? We could count incorrectly spelled words, incorrect punctuation, or examples of inconsistent tense, but otherwise we might as well grit our teeth and admit that the criteria are extremely subjective. Scoring these questions is a more time-consuming process and is more susceptible to error than is objective scoring.

In fact, most states use written general criteria (such as "logical development of ideas" and "clear expression of thoughts"). Most also use teams of scorers who have been thoroughly trained in how to score the responses, so that each short-answer and essay question is scored by more than one person. Such practices can lower the likelihood of variability among scorers, but they cannot eliminate them. So test makers would say that scores on short-answer and essay questions are less *reliable* than objectively scored questions.

Subject Areas

The days when standardized tests only asked questions about word recognition, spelling, and arithmetic are long gone. Today, tests assess many different subjects. Some standardized test publishers offer modular systems with a core test of reading, spelling, and math questions; school districts can then add other components, such as study skills, social studies, or science. Other tests come with prepackaged components, and school districts use all components or none of them.

Nevertheless, there are some subjects that all students who take standardized tests will commonly encounter. Let's look at some of the subjects that standardized tests will assess.

Reading

Reading is guaranteed to be on every standardized test. Tests generally assess both *letter-word identification* and *reading comprehension.* Letter-word identification may go by other names such as *basic reading skill* or *word recognition.* It involves the ability to identify letters or words.

Depending on the age of the students assessed, this section of tests will present letters or words and ask students to identify them. For example:

---

1   Which picture goes with the letter f̲?

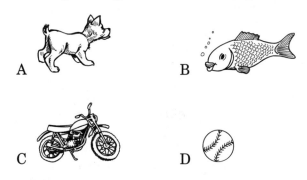

A   B

C   D

[Answer: B]

Reading comprehension refers to the ability to understand the meaning of a written passage. This skill requires your child to recognize words and also to piece together the different elements to understand the whole meaning.

Reading comprehension is the ability to understand the meaning of all those separate words when they are combined in a certain way. Sometimes (especially with older students) reading comprehension questions will require the student to read the passage and draw conclusions. For example:

2   Oeshaun was walking in the woods when he saw a
    pretty plant growing up a tree. He picked the leaves
    and carried them home to show his mother. When
    she saw the leaves, she became upset and told
    Oeshaun to put them in the garbage. She made
    Oeshaun take a bath and change his clothes. The
    next day, he broke out with a rash all over his body.
    He itched terribly. He had to go to the doctor and get
    medicine to help him feel better. What plant did
    Oeshaun pick in the woods?

A daffodils

B holly leaves

C roses

D poison ivy

[Answer: D]

Math

Most standardized tests assess *mathematics calculation* and
mathematics reasoning. Mathematics calculation may go
by different names, such as *mathematics operations* or
basic mathematics.

In early grades, the tests try to determine whether students understand basic mathematical symbols and can perform simple addition and subtraction. In later elementary
grades, questions will require students to multiply and
divide. By late high school, questions may include complex
algebra, calculus, and trigonometry.

Mathematics calculation items are usually very straightforward. The biggest problem that students encounter with
such questions, other than simply not knowing how to do
the calculations, is not paying attention. Some students don't

pay attention to the signs of operation and answer "3 × 5" as if it were "3 + 5." Other children rush through without taking the time to think about their answers.

Mathematics reasoning goes a step beyond simple calculation and usually involves word problems. To answer a word problem, a child must read the problem and understand the steps involved in solving it. For instance:

---

1 Sung Duk invited his friends Bill and Ahmed to go to the zoo with him. If tickets for children are $4.00 each, how much did all three boys' tickets cost?

For students to solve this problem, they must be able to translate the problem into a math calculation problem, multiplying 3 boys times $4.00 each. To solve such problems, students not only must be able to perform the necessary calculations, but must be able to understand the elements of the question.

Many students don't know how to read figures such as bar charts, pie charts, or graphs. Others pay only scant attention to them and don't glean the information from them that they need to accurately work the problem. Students must take the time to thoroughly read the questions and study any accompanying graphics to help solve the problems.

Spelling

It's odd that adults who would be ashamed to admit they couldn't read will freely admit to an inability to spell. Spelling ability is difficult to assess with most standardized tests because those tests use multiple-choice questions. At most, such questions only assess how well children can recognize correct spelling, not whether they can produce correct spelling from memory. In many classrooms, this lack of emphasis on recall spelling has resulted in a de-emphasis on such skills in the classroom.

Students are most likely to encounter questions such as these:

---

1   In the produce section of a grocery store you can usually find a ____?
    A cantalope
    B cantellope
    C cantilope
    D cantaloupe

[Answer: D]

2   In the spring Vanessa liked to pick _____.
    A daffydills
    B dafodills
    C daffodils
    D daphodyls

[Answer: C]

It is on a criterion-referenced test that students are most likely to answer spelling questions that test their ability to recall the correct spelling. However, it's hard to come up with questions to elicit correct answers. For example, the question "How do you spell the word for car that is pronounced aw-to-mo-bill?" presents a problem in that the phonetic spelling of the pronunciation gives the student valuable hints about how to spell the word. If we present a picture of a mountain and ask "How do you spell what is in the picture?" students might not understand that the word we are looking for is *mountain* and may spell *p-e-a-k.*

More commonly, criterion-referenced tests will assess recall spelling by having the proctor dictate the words.

Language

Language sections (also called language mechanics or communication) include *testing of grammar and sentence construction, vocabulary, expression, and listening comprehension.* Grammar and sentence-construction questions try to determine whether students have mastered the rules for statement construction. For example, a test may ask:

---

1   Choose the correct sentence.

   A Johnny does not have any money.

   B Johnny ain't got no money.

   C Johnny does not have no money.

   D Johnny has none money.

[Answer: A]

2   Choose the correct word to go in the blank.

   Tammy likes to visit her friend Juan. Yesterday, she
   _____ to Juan's house.

   A goed

   B go'd

   C wented

   D went

[Answer: D]

Grammar and sentence-construction questions on criterion-referenced tests will frequently resemble these:

---

3   Fill in the blank in each of the following sentences
    with a correct word.
    Maria was born on April 12. Helmut was _____
    on the same day.
[Answer: born]
    Caroline _____ down the street after her
    puppy.
[Answer: ran; walked; sprinted; trotted]

Note that in these examples, the student must recall the
correct form of a word. Now look at these examples:

---

4   Rewrite these sentences so that they are correct.
    Lakeisha, was the First in line she paid her. Money
    and go'd into the movie.
[Answer: Lakeisha was the first in line. She paid her
money and went into the movie.]

The advantage of this type of question is that it can
assess the student's knowledge of several elements of grammar and sentence construction at the same time, including
tense, capitalization, and placement of punctuation.

Vocabulary refers to the repertoire of words that students use or understand. A question gauging this skill, more
typically found on criterion-referenced tests, may resemble
the following:

---

5   Write the word that means to determine how long a
    piece of wood is by using a yardstick.

[Answer: measure]

6   What word means a piece of wood used to hit a
    baseball?

[Answer: bat]

The term *receptive vocabulary* refers to words that students recognize and understand. For example:

---

7   Look at the pictures below. Choose the picture of a
     <u>canine</u>.

A   B

C   D

[Answer: A]

8   Which word means <u>to work with someone after
     school to help them learn better</u>?
     A cipher
     B tutor
     C coagulate
     D regulate

[Answer: B]

Notice that this type of question only requires students to recognize the word when they see it. It requires only a superficial knowledge of vocabulary. Your child's performance on such questions only estimates her ability to understand the vocabulary that others use. It doesn't say anything about the quality of the vocabulary that they use. The above questions are typical of the major commercial group standardized tests because they lend themselves very readily to machine scoring.

Language expression is very difficult to assess on tests that require multiple-choice questions. Short-answer and essay questions are more appropriate for gauging this skill, but these questions require a subjective scoring of student responses and can't be scored by machine. Language-expression questions are rare on norm-referenced tests, which almost always demand multiple-choice questions.

The most common subset of language expression that criterion-referenced tests assess is written expression; most use a combination of short-answer and essay questions such as these:

[short answer]

9   Write a complete sentence giving one reason why children should not accept rides from strangers.

[Criterion: Any grammatically correct sentence giving a plausible reason.]

[essay]

10 In one page or less, describe your favorite memory.

The advantage of short-answer and essay questions in assessing written expression is that they give the student an opportunity to demonstrate a much deeper level of skills than do multiple-choice tests. By completing short-answer questions, students can show that they can construct proper sentences that actually make sense. By completing essay questions, students can show not only a basic understanding but information analysis and synthesis.

Listening comprehension requires that students listen to someone read a passage, discriminate essential from nonessential details, and reconstruct the meaning of the passages. In the past, standardized tests didn't include listening comprehension questions because they require an extra step of having a test proctor read passages or play a prerecorded tape.

The test typically asks one or two questions on shorter passages, and more with longer samples. Here are two examples of listening comprehension questions:

[short passage read to the students]

11 Nibbles lives in a cage in Ross's bedroom. He sleeps during the day and runs on his wheel all night. He likes to eat peanuts. Grandmother Steele is afraid to pick him up. What kind of animal could Nibbles be?

[Acceptable answers: hamster, mouse, gerbil]

[long passage read to the students]

Bill moved from the big city to the country. He looked around for a park to play in, but there were no parks nearby. All his friends had nice, big yards to play in, and there were woods with creeks and ponds to explore. One day, when Bill and his friends were playing at Fletcher's Pond, Bill's friend Heyward fell into the pond and began to scream for help. Anna, Heyward's sister, screamed, "He can't swim! Save him!"

Bill had taken lifeguard lessons when he lived in the city. He jumped into the pond and swam over to Heyward. Heyward was scared and tried to fight, but fortunately Bill was ready for this. Bill's lifeguard instructor had taught him that people who can't swim and who fall into water usually fight those who try to save them. Bill knew how to grab Heyward from behind, and he swam back to shore with him. Heyward was all right, but his mother took Anna and him to the YMCA the next day to sign them up for swimming lessons.

12 Bill moved <u>from</u> where <u>to</u> where?
  A from the country to the city
  B from Europe to the United States
  C from Mexico to Texas
  D from the city to the country

[Answer: D]

13 Why were there no parks to play in where Bill moved?
  A He and the other children he knew all had big yards to play in.
  B There were parks, but his mother would not allow him to play in them.
  C The city council where he moved would not approve the money for parks.
  D There was no room to build a park because there were too many houses.

[Answer: A]

14 What happened to the boy who fell into the pond?
  A He drowned.
  B Bill rescued him.
  C Bill ran for help, and Mr. Fletcher jumped in and saved him.
  D He found a rock and managed to climb up on it.

[Answer: B]

Other Subjects

Most norm-referenced and criterion-referenced tests provide additional testing that varies from test to test. Several of the major standardized tests offer these additional tests in modular packages that school districts can elect to buy or not. Two of the more common additional test areas are *science* and *social studies.*

Science test questions, depending on the grade level of the students, will assess a wide range of knowledge including earth science, physical science, chemistry, and physics. Science is a subject that allows the full use of multiple-choice, short-answer, and essay questions. Most norm-referenced tests use multiple-choice questions, and criterion-referenced tests use a mixture of multiple-choice, short-answer, and essay questions.

Typical science questions would resemble these examples:

---

1   In the formula for water, H_2O, what do the $\underline{H}$ and the $\underline{O}$ represent?
   A helium and oxygen
   B hydrogen and organase
   C hydrogen and oxygen
   D helium and organase

[Answer: C]

2   Where is the Orion Nebula located?

[Answer: in the belt in the Orion constellation]

3   In one page or less, describe the stages of develop-
    ment of a baby from conception to birth. Use dia-
    grams if you think they help.

As with science, social studies lends itself very well to
the whole range of question types, including multiple-
choice, short-answer, and essay questions. They assess not
only factual understanding but, depending on the grade
level of the students being tested, the ability to read maps
and understand such complex concepts as political trends,
emigration patterns, and controversies.

For example:

---

1   Who conquered the British Isles in 1066?
    A   William the Bruce
    B   William the Conqueror
    C   Crazy William
    D   Kaiser Wilhelm

[Answer: B]

2   What was the *Hunley*?

[Answer: The first submarine to sink an enemy ship.
It was built during the Civil War and sank in the har-
bor in Charleston, South Carolina.]

3   In one page or less, describe the main events that
    led to World War I.

At higher grade levels, students will be asked to demonstrate their ability to reason and infer, such as is represented
by the following question:

4   In your opinion, was the Civil War fought over slav-
    ery? Justify your answer in one page or less.

Summary

Questions on standardized tests fall into one of two major
categories: recognition questions (most often represented
by multiple-choice questions) that require the test taker to
recognize the correct answer among two or more alternatives (usually four or five) and recall questions (represented
by short-answer and essay questions) that require the test
taker to actively retrieve information from memory.

Recognition questions require a more superficial mastery of subject matter, but they can be objectively scored by
computers, answer key overlays, or optical scanning sheets.
Compared with recognition questions, recall questions
require the student to demonstrate a deeper mastery of subjects, but recall questions can't be scored by machine.
Unlike scoring the answers to recognition questions, scoring
the answers to recall questions is subjective.

The major subject areas of test questions on standardized tests include reading, math, spelling, language, and others such as social studies and science.

Decoding Your Child's Score

When you read the title of this chapter, you probably had an urge to quickly flip to another section—but don't! Understanding your child's test scores is much easier than most people think.

And since interpretations and misinterpretations of your child's scores dictate how the schools will use the test results, it's essential for you to read on. In this chapter, you'll learn about the most important statistical concept involved in testing—the bell curve.

The Bell Curve: It's Not as Hard as You Think

The bell curve is simply a graph of how often something tends to occur. For example, the graph in Figure 3-1 shows how often "heads" occurred when students threw groups of 10 pennies 1000 times.

Figure 3-1   Typical Bell Curve

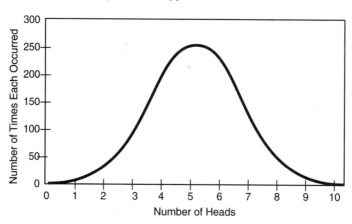

Notice that the graph looks sort of like a bell—hence the name *bell curve.* Also note that most of the "heads" are in the middle of the range, and the farther we move away from the middle, the fewer number of trials there are with that number of heads.

You will find that we come up with a bell curve when we look at many different types of things, such as:

- The number of ice cream cones per day people buy at an amusement park
- The speeds that cars travel down the interstate highway between 2 p.m. and 3 p.m. each day
- The heights and weights of women shopping at the local mall
- The distance between people's eyes
- The number of feet children can kick a soccer ball

In each of these examples, if you graphed the number of times each value occurred, you'd see that most of the values would be close to the average, and the fewest would fall near the two extremes.

One of the basic assumptions behind educational and psychological testing is that students' test scores fall along a bell curve. To interpret scores on a test, we need to understand two concepts related to the bell curve: the mean and percentile.

The Mean (Average)

The average is important because it gives us a way of comparing one score with the other scores in a group. If Linda brings home a test score of 85, for example, we can't determine whether that is a good score until we know the average. If the average is 500, an 85 would be terrible; but if the average is 50, an 85 would be quite good.

Percentile

Even if we know the average, we still need to know something about how often each score occurs. Another important statistical term that psychologists use to describe test scores is the *cumulative percent*—also known as the *percentile*. Very simply, the percentile is the percentage of scores equal to or below a certain score.

To illustrate this, let's go back to our example of Linda, who had a test score of 85. If 78 percent of the scores on the test that Linda took fell at or below 85, we would say that the percentile of Linda's score percentile is 78—the 78th percentile. So, if you know the percentile, you can tell how your child's score ranks among other scores.

You will see different guidelines for how to interpret scores depending on the test, and some are more useful than others. Table 3-1 shows one way to interpret percentiles on any test.

Table 3-1   Interpreting Percentiles

Percentile Range	Level
2 and below	Deficient
3–8	Borderline
9–23	Low average
24–75	Average
76–97	High average
98 and above	Superior

Many people are surprised to learn how wide the average range is. Most school psychologists have had to deal with parents who panicked when their child made a score somewhere around the 27th percentile. But you can see from Table 3-1 that the 27th percentile is actually in the average range.

Congratulations! You now know everything you need to know for a basic interpretation of test scores. So let's apply what we have learned with a real-life test score report.

Interpretation of Test Reports

Let's look at a sample test report that's similar to one you might receive after your child's testing. In this case, we'll use sample test score reports from the TerraNova. If your child takes a different standardized test, the report may look slightly different, but the TerraNova report contains the basic type of information you can expect to receive.

Look at Figure 3-2. This bar chart presents of scores for fictitious student Mary Brown. On the left side of the graph, a scale gives the national percentiles for the scores. On the right, bracketed areas give parents a quick, rough interpretation of the scores. In this case, note that almost all of Mary's scores are within the average range, while math and spelling are above average.

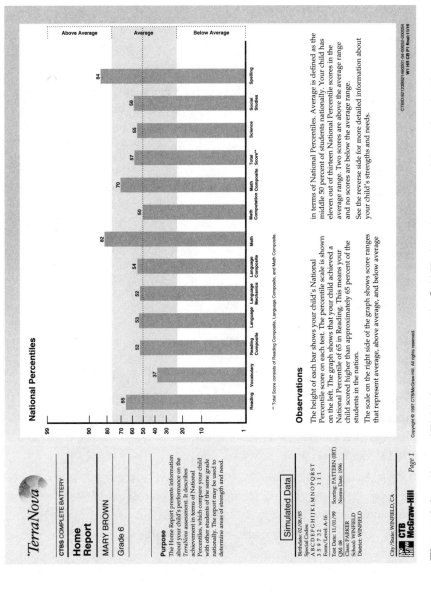

Figure 3-2 (*Source:* CTB/McGraw-Hill, copyright © 1997. All rights reserved. Reproduced with permission.)

65

The kind of information in this graph may be rough, but it does give parents a simple way of comparing their child's scores. Figure 3-3 interprets Mary Brown's scores a slightly different way, by showing general level of skill mastery for each area tested.

In this figure, look near the bottom just above "General Interpretation" to find a key to interpreting the circle next to each area of testing, indicating that Mary has shown mastery, partial mastery, or nonmastery of each skill area. Note that this report breaks down each scale into the subskills tested. For the most part, Mary has mastered the skills tested. But if you look in the "Needs" column, you will see that she has shown only partial mastery of "evaluate and extend meaning" under Reading, "writing strategies" under "Language," "measurement" and "geometry and spatial sense" under Mathematics, and "historical and cultural perspectives" under Social Studies.

"Partial mastery" means that she is part of the way toward mastering those skills but is not yet competent in them. She tested at a nonmastery level in "identify reading strategies" under "Reading," "multimeaning words" under "Vocabulary," "writing conventions" under "Language Mechanics," "percents" under "Mathematics Computation," and "earth and space science" under "Science."

The interpretation provided in this figure is somewhat rough. And keep in mind the cautions offered later in Chapter 7 about applying results of group standardized tests with individuals. Use the information in this figure as a guide, but don't make a detailed diagnosis of an individual student's learning problems.

Figure 3-4 is perhaps the most useful report for teachers and parents who know how to interpret the information there. Let's start with the table at the top of the report. Look

°TerraNova

CTBS COMPLETE BATTERY

Home Report

MARY BROWN

Grade 6

Purpose

This page of the Home Report presents information about your child's strengths and needs. This information is provided to help you monitor your child's academic growth.

Simulated Data

Birthdate: 02/08/85
Special Codes:
A B C D E F G H I J K L M N O P Q R S T
3 5 9 7 3 2   1 1 1
Form/Level: A-16
Test Date: 11/01/99   Scoring: PATTERN (IRT)
QM: 08   Norms Date: 1996

Class: PARKER
School: WINFIELD
District: WINFIELD

City/State: WINFIELD, CA

CTB McGraw-Hill

Page 2

Strengths

Reading
● Basic Understanding
● Analyze Text

Vocabulary
● Word Meaning
● Words in Context

Language
● Editing Skills
● Sentence Structure

Language Mechanics
● Sentences, Phrases, Clauses

Mathematics
● Computation and Numerical Estimation
● Operation Concepts

Mathematics Computation
● Add Whole Numbers
● Multiply Whole Numbers

Science
● Life Science
● Inquiry Skills

Social Studies
● Geographic Perspectives
● Economic Perspectives

Spelling
● Vowels
● Consonants

Key ● **Mastery**

General Interpretation

The left column shows your child's best areas of performance. In each case, your child has reached mastery level. The column at the right shows the areas within each test section where your child's scores are the lowest. In these cases, your child has not reached mastery level, although he or she may have reached partial mastery.

Copyright © 1997 CTB/McGraw-Hill. All rights reserved.

Needs

Reading
◑ Evaluate and Extend Meaning
○ Identify Reading Strategies

Vocabulary
○ Multimeaning Words

Language
◑ Writing Strategies

Language Mechanics
○ Writing Conventions

Mathematics
◑ Measurement
◑ Geometry and Spatial Sense

Mathematics Computation
○ Percents

Science
○ Earth and Space Science

Social Studies
◑ Historical and Cultural Perspectives

Spelling
No area of needs were identified for this content area

Key ◑ **Partial Mastery**   ○ **Non-Mastery**

CTBID:92123882146I0001-04-00052-000054
W1 CB HR P2 Final:11005

Figure 3-3   (*Source:* CTB/McGraw-Hill, copyright © 1997. All rights reserved. Reproduced with permission.)

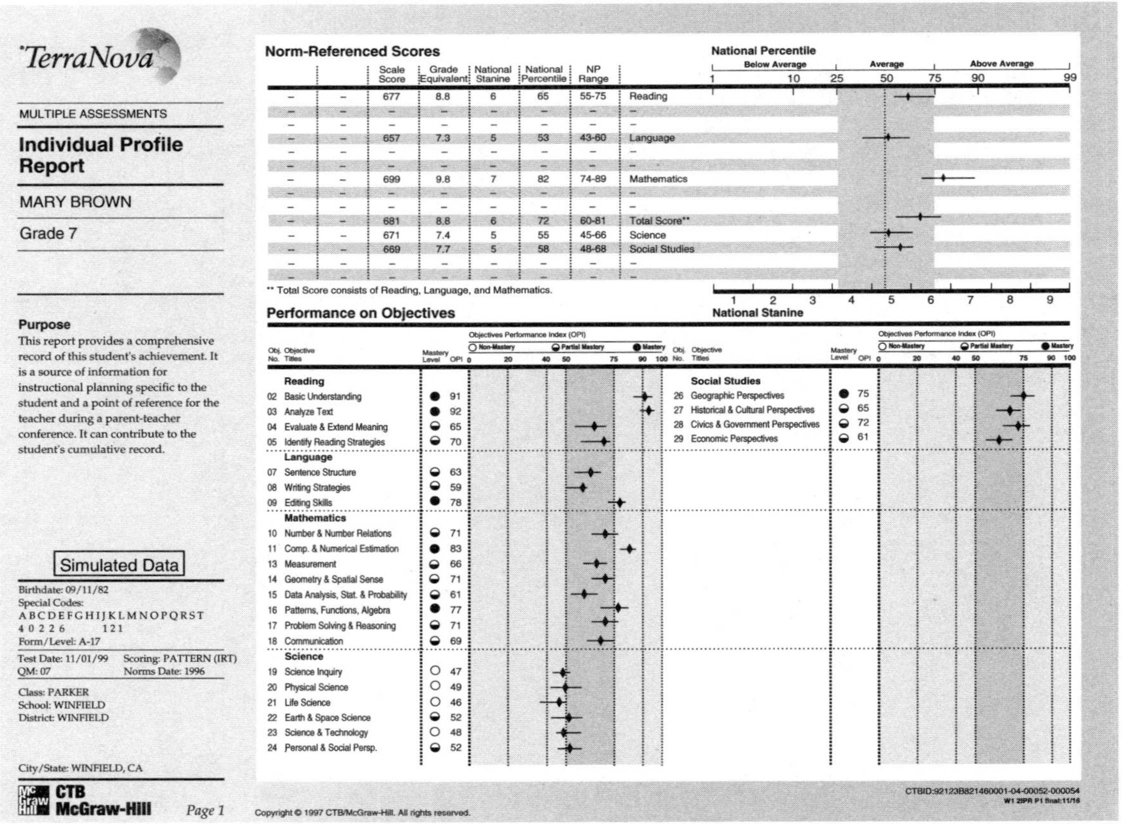

Figure 3-4 (Source: CTB/McGraw-Hill, copyright © 1997. All rights reserved. Reproduced ith permission.)

at the column labeled "National Percentile." This is exactly the same thing we referred to above. "National" means that the percentile score refers to the percentage of scores at or below the score in a national sample. A national percentile (which is frequently abbreviated "NP") of 45, for example, means that an estimated 45 percent of students from all over the United States would score at or below this score.

Although not used in this figure, you might sometimes come across the term *local percentile* (frequently abbreviated "LP"). This term refers to the percentage of students locally (such as within the state, school district, or even individual school) who scored at or below the score. Use Table 3-1 (in the "Percentile" section) to interpret the national percentile for each scale's score.

The next column is labeled "NP Range," which means "national percentile range." All scores vary. For example, if a child takes the same test more than once, it is likely she will make different scores on different days. A number of factors, such as whether the child is excited about an upcoming school vacation, how well the child feels on a given day, how noisy it is outside the classroom, and so on, can affect that student's scores. All of us recall information with different levels of accuracy from one day to the next. *NP range* refers to the range in which we would expect the child's percentiles to fall a certain amount of the time if the child could take the same test more than once.

Now look at the graph to the right of the score table at the top of the report. Rather than report the student's score as a single point, a large dot represents the actual score with lines extending to the left and to the right indicating the NP range. This way of graphing a student's scores gives a much better idea of how precise an individual score is.

There are other scores in the table at the top of this report, but you already have all the information you need to interpret them. Don't worry about the columns labeled "Scale Score" and "National Stanine." These refer to more specialized statistical scores. Once you know how to interpret percentiles, you don't need to worry about scaled scores or stanines.

There is a column we have ignored up to this point, labeled "Grade Equivalent." The temptation here is to simply advise you to ignore that column. But the truth is that your child's teacher, administrators, and counselors will make such a fuss about grade equivalents that you need to know something about them. Psychologists believe that grade equivalents are very misleading.

Technically, a grade equivalent is supposed to refer to the average grade of all the students who made a certain score. Mary Brown's grade equivalent of 8:8 in reading supposedly means that Mary is reading at the 8th month of the 8th grade level.

The biggest problem with grade equivalents is that the way we determine them varies from test to test. The same score, for example, may be 8:8 on one test, 12:6 on another, and 13:2 on yet another. One test may calculate grade equivalents by some obscure formula. Another test may calculate grade equivalents by determining the average grade placement of all the students who made a certain score.

Another big problem with grade equivalents is that they can give a false sense of where the student is actually functioning. On one major test, for example, the average reading level for high school seniors in the final month of high school is 8:0 rather than the expected 12:9. That doesn't mean that the average high school senior is reading nearly five grade levels behind but rather that the way the test publisher calculates grade equivalents is very misleading at the upper grades.

Regardless of how much others may emphasize grade equivalents, refer to Table 3-1 and interpret percentiles and ignore the grade equivalents. If someone makes a fuss about your child's grade equivalents, refer that person to the percentiles.

Now look at the bottom two-thirds of Figure 3-4, where we see Mary Brown's degree of mastery on the different skill areas. The interpretation here is very straightforward, just like the skills breakdown in Figure 3-3.

Notice the column labeled "OPI." This refers to the Objective Performance Index. The OPI is an estimate of the percentage of items the student should be able to answer correctly for each skill area. An OPI of 23 for a certain skill area, for example, means that we estimate that the student would be able to correctly answer 23 percent of the items for that skill. That gives a rough idea of how proficient the student is in that skill.

On the TerraNova, an OPI of 75 or above signifies mastery, an OPI between 50 and 74 signifies partial mastery, and an OPI below 50 indicates nonmastery.

After the Dust Settles: What You Can Do

So the big day has finally arrived: The newspapers run charts and graphs showing the standardized test scores for the schools in your area. Your son comes home with that cryptic printout that we learned to interpret in Chapter 3.

You know from what you've already read in this book that group standardized tests aren't designed to diagnose individual students. But that little irrational voice inside your head can't help making a big fuss over the fact that your son's reading score is dismal. Or perhaps your son's teacher told you that your son's low group aptitude score is the same thing as an IQ (it isn't). Of course you react emotionally and begin to wonder if maybe there's a problem you didn't suspect. You're not alone.

Yvonne was a popular class leader who made A's and B's in all her subjects. Her teacher could always depend on Yvonne, who finished her homework every day without complaint. On the rare occasions Yvonne needed help with her homework, she caught on quickly. But her parents scheduled a meeting with the teacher to express anguish over the fact that her standardized test report showed a very low reading score. Her parents thought perhaps Yvonne needed a tutorial reading program.

Fortunately, Yvonne's school district doesn't automatically assign students with low standardized test scores to the tutorial reading program, but lets parents and teachers make decisions based on the overall picture. When Yvonne's parents and teacher met and reviewed Yvonne's homework, class work, class test grades, and special projects, it was clear that she was doing fine. In fact, the only thing about Yvonne that anyone could fault was her low reading score on the most recent group standardized test.

So instead of putting her in a tutoring program, her parents and teacher paid special attention to Yvonne's progress in reading group and monitored her reading at home over the next several weeks, and no one saw a problem in her reading. They decided she did not need extra help.

On the other hand, Michael had a history of problems in all subjects. His teachers had always noted that he didn't learn new skills well and that his homework and class work were full of errors. He seemed unhappy and totally lost in class. His parents struggled to help him understand his homework, but often he just didn't get it.

His standardized test scores had always been dismal, and the latest round of results was no exception. Michael's parents and teacher decided to refer him to the child study team at his school to try to determine what they needed to do for Michael.

After a series of unsuccessful interventions, the school psychologist found that Michael had a learning disability in basic reading skill, reading comprehension, mathematics calculation, and mathematics reasoning. He was placed in the district's handicapped program with an Individualized Education Program and began receiving two periods of resource classes each day.

The above examples show that test scores have to be evaluated in perspective. Still, in many school districts, your child will nevertheless be judged, diagnosed, and classified by standardized test scores, whether it's valid to do so or not.

Many schools still use those scores to place students unnecessarily in remedial programs or deny entrance into prestigious programs for the gifted. This is why you should understand what your child's test scores mean, how the school district might use them, and what to do if the scores support your suspicion that your child has a learning problem. In this chapter, you'll learn what to do when the scores arrive, how to see if your child might have a learning problem, and how to get help if there is a problem.

Is There a Problem?

You've got your child's test scores. You've read in Chapter 3 how to interpret test results, and you realize that his math scores are very low. You recall that he seemed healthy when the tests had been given, so the low scores probably can't be blamed on illness. The first thing you need to do is sit down with your spouse and discuss the situation.

Think back to the times you both helped your child with schoolwork. Did he seem to struggle with certain concepts? Did he come home from school upset because he just couldn't understand the new information the teacher presented? Perhaps he referred to himself in derogatory terms, such as "dummy."

Look back over past schoolwork. Are there any patterns that hint of a possible learning problem? Maybe your child does well with simple math problems, but completely falls apart when it comes to regrouping (what you think of as "carrying" or "borrowing"). If it's spelling that's the problem, maybe your child consistently misspells words that have more than two syllables, or often mispronounces words.

Next, check with your child. Does he think there's a problem? Children can be astute observers of their own behavior and often have great insight into their own problems. Maybe your child thinks everything is all right—or that most things are okay, but he has trouble reading: Perhaps he complains that he can identify each word, but has problems following along with and understanding what the passages say. Maybe he can't see the board or can't hear the teacher, and you suspect a vision or a hearing problem. It could be that a visit to the ophthalmologist or audiologist will make a world of difference. If so, terrific. But if it's not as easily solved as that, you may need to look farther.

Your Child's Teacher

Your child's teacher is a great resource and can be your best friend when it comes to identifying your child's learning problems and to developing strategies for dealing with those problems. Teachers can often reassure parents that the situation isn't as bleak as it may seem.

You may be the expert on your child, but your child's teacher has probably seen hundreds of students in her career. Many teachers have a keen eye for who's having a problem and who isn't. The teacher can review your child's performance, and can show you how he's doing compared with the other students. Your child's portfolio can be very valuable in showing how your child is actually performing in school every day, regardless of what the test scores say.

The teacher can also shed light on something you probably don't get to see every day—how well your child works in class. She can tell you whether your child fidgets and squirms and whether he has friends in the class. She can comment on whether he seems to enjoy school or if he is frustrated and withdrawn. Sometimes the teacher is the first one to note a developing emotional problem.

Your child's teacher can also tell you what will happen to your child as a result of any unusual test scores. As you talk with the teacher, keep in mind that teachers typically have no input in how the school district will use the test scores—they are just the messengers.

Does your school district automatically place low-scoring students into remedial programs? If so, can you appeal? Is there a risk that your child might need to repeat a grade because of low standardized test scores? In some school districts, your child's low scores may lead to failing a grade or being denied a diploma, regardless of report card grades and teachers' judgments about how well he's doing in school.

Guidance Counselor

Your next step in discovering if your child has learning problems is to go to your child's guidance counselor. Most guidance counselors have been classroom teachers and not only have the perspective of a veteran teacher but are usually trained in test interpretation and student services. Although a counselor won't usually have firsthand knowledge of your child's performance in the classroom, she'll be able to look at your child's record and can advise you about the possibility of a learning problem. The guidance counselor will have available the scores of the other students in your child's class and grade and can give you a quick judgment of just where your child's scores fit in with the others.

Child Study Team

Let's suppose that you've been to the teacher and to the guidance counselor and you're still not happy. Maybe you see a problem where they don't, or perhaps you disagree about how to address your child's difficulties. Or perhaps you, the teacher, and the guidance counselor have tried everything—and your child is still struggling.

You may want to consider utilizing your school's *child study team,* whose function is to identify children who need some sort of special help, to decide what help to offer, and to refer children for more testing when needed. The teams may go by other names in your child's school, such as *student assistance team* or *student intervention team,* but they all function the same way: They review information from parents, school records, previous and current teachers, and the child. The group, which may also include both parents and teachers, meet and discuss the child's problems and potential strategies to help the child. They may even involve the student in strategy sessions to come up with appropriate ways to overcome the problems.

There are several ways that you can involve a child study team. Usually, your child's teacher would notify the team coordinator—probably a guidance counselor, special education teacher, or assistant principal. Sometimes counselors or administrators ask the team to consider a child's problems. But you can refer your child, too. Ask your child's teacher what specific steps you need to take at your school to have the team help with your child. If the teacher doesn't know, ask the guidance counselor. Check out the student handbook for information on accessing the child study team.

Working with a child study team is a great way for you to get involved with your child's education in a very direct and meaningful way. It may be inconvenient to leave work to attend the strategy meetings, but go to every meeting you can. Do your homework: Come in with suggestions, materials, notes about sessions between you and your child, and any other information you think might help. You'll find that the child study team will welcome your involvement with open arms.

The child study team will assign various team members, sometimes including you and your spouse, with tasks to help your child. For example, the team might ask that you drill your child for 20 minutes a day on spelling words or that you review basic addition and subtraction for 30 minutes a day using flash cards. Perhaps the team might ask you to read over your child's writing assignments to check for spelling and punctuation errors. If the team asks you to take part of the responsibility for helping your child, rejoice! It obviously has faith in your ability to help. The team members aren't pushing their responsibilities off on you; they're giving you the chance to be involved in your child's education.

Once everyone has been working on the strategy to help your child for a period of time, the child study team will meet again to review the results. Usually your child will have made progress. If not, team members will discuss new ideas. Sometimes finding out what doesn't work is an important first step to success.

This process could go on for some time as the team fine-tunes a specific program for your child, and many times it is successful. Sometimes, however, the team members realize they've reached a dead end. If the child is still struggling, the team may decide to call for a special education evaluation.

The focus of the special education evaluation is to determine whether your child qualifies for any of the 13 handicaps defined in the federal law governing special education, called the Individuals with Disabilities Education Act (IDEA). These handicaps include:

- Autism
- Deaf-blindness
- Deafness
- Hearing problems
- Mental retardation
- Multiple disabilities
- Orthopedic problems
- Other health problems such as having strength or alertness difficulties affecting school performance
- Serious emotional disturbance
- Specific learning disability
- Speech or language problems
- Traumatic brain injury
- Eye problems, including blindness

By the time the child study team begins a special education evaluation, team members will have a tremendous amount of information about your child far beyond standardized test scores. They will have samples of his daily work, details about what strategies did and didn't work, and health screenings to rule out hearing or eye problems. They will have a thorough description of the types of problems your child has every day.

But they may need the input of other professionals. Depending on the specific nature of your child's problems, various professionals may help with this special education evaluation, such as:

• Speech and language therapist
• School psychologist
• Audiologist
• Hearing education teacher
• Special education teacher
• Physician

The evaluation that will determine whether your child will qualify for consideration for special education placement will probably involve assessments by several of these specialists. At the very least, the school psychologist, the referring teacher, and a speech-language pathologist usually will complete the needed evaluations.

Note that the evaluation by itself simply determines whether the child study team may consider your child for placement in special education, since the team may only consider children for special education placement if they meet certain requirements.

Special Education Placement

Suppose the child study team now has sufficient information to recommend assembling a placement team to consider placing your child in the district's handicapped program. A complete discussion of the placement options and all of the ins and outs of special education placement is beyond the scope of this book. But it's important to understand that if your child enters special education, the school will provide an Individualized Education Program (IEP), which governs all aspects of your child's educational program.

If There's a Learning Problem

If your child does appear to have a significant learning problem, the teacher can help you learn what to do about it, suggesting reading books, workbooks, and other material that will be similar to those your child sees in class. For example, many textbooks have companion workbooks that school districts don't order because of the cost. So if your child is having a problem in, say, math, there may be a companion workbook to his math book you can order.

The teacher also can give you a schedule of upcoming curriculum topics so that you can plan your work at home around that schedule. Teachers can send home supplemental materials and provide advice about educational software that parallels what your child is learning in the classroom.

Sometimes the teacher just doesn't know whether there is a problem. Perhaps she's a substitute who only recently took over the class and who hasn't known your child long enough to be able to give you any meaningful information. Or maybe your child has a new teacher who doesn't have the experience to be able to spot children with problems. Sometimes, you and the teacher just don't get along—or perhaps you have seen the teacher and you're just not satisfied with her response.

Get a Tutor

If your child doesn't qualify for special education, he may qualify for remedial services. For example, if your child has been struggling with reading, he may qualify for placement in a tutorial reading program which he attends one hour every day. Most schools offer such programs, and you may find that a few months or more in this program will bring your child's reading up to an appropriate level, and he can stop attending the classes.

If your child is still struggling in school but doesn't qualify for special education or for the school's remedial program, you may have to go outside the school to obtain a tutor. Sometimes, you can find private tutors whose rates are reasonable. Talk to your friends and get recommendations, or call your child's school and ask for recommendations. Check out the community bulletin board at your local grocery store for tutor services, or visit your local library. There are many retired teachers who tutor a few students for extra income. These individuals bring many years of experience to help your child and can sometimes work wonders. Most veteran teachers have enough experience that they can advise you if the problem is too serious for them to handle.

College students (especially those studying to be teachers) are another good tutoring choice. Call your local college's teacher education program and ask for recommendations. Some colleges maintain registers of students who are looking for jobs as tutors. One of the great advantages of college students is their enthusiasm. Since they are in training, they probably are familiar with the most modern materials and texts. Regularly employed teachers also work as tutors outside of school hours.

If you can't afford a private tutor, you might check at your church or the local community center. Many have volunteers who devote one or more afternoons a week to tutoring. Organizations such as the YMCA, YWCA, and Boys and Girls Clubs have free or low-cost after-school tutorial programs as well.

Alternatively, you may want to consider commercial tutorial services such as the Sylvan Learning Centers (1-888-

EDUCATE or www.educate.com), which provide diagnostic and tutorial services after school, during summers, and on the weekends. Such services offer a range of possible programs that include tutoring in specific areas or general study skills, listening, and note taking. Don't forget to consult the Yellow Pages under "Educational Consultants," "Educational Services," or "Tutorial Services."

Another recent development, borrowed from similar programs in Japan and Korea, is the Saturday school. These schools provide after-school and weekend educational services meant to reinforce children's learning and to treat any specific problems. While not widely available, they are becoming more common in larger metropolitan areas.

Advocacy

You've learned what to do if low standardized test scores point to a real learning problem your child may have. But what if you, your child, and your child's teacher believe that despite low scores, your child is doing well in school. If your school district enforces policies that penalize your child in some way for those low test scores, it may be time for some good old-fashioned advocacy.

Perhaps your child's school district requires that students with low test scores automatically repeat grades or are denied diplomas. That is the very challenge that parents in one North Carolina school district and another in Texas faced when their children were told they must repeat their grades, even though their report card grades had been strong and their teachers had judged them to have learned appropriately. In these cases, the policies in place did not give the parents any input into whether their children would repeat their grades or fail to graduate, and the teachers and principals were powerless to intervene, even when they considered the consequences to be unreasonable.

You will find that it is easier to dispute local policies that are unique to your child's school than to fight a policy that has been mandated by your school district. And you'll have better luck fighting policies mandated by your state department of public instruction than you will fighting national policies.

Local Policies

If there is a local policy at your child's school or school district that inappropriately uses group standardized test scores, your first step will be to determine who at the school is responsible for the testing program. This person is usually an assistant principal or guidance counselor.

Talk to that person and find out just how much room there is for change. For example, if the policy requires your child to repeat her grade on the basis of her standardized test scores but she's doing well in school otherwise, is there a way to either retest her or make an individual exception?

If not, you'll have to go to the principal, and from there to the district's assistant superintendent for instruction, and from there to the superintendent and the school board.

If you get as far as an appeal before the school board, you should get some help—preferably backup by other parents who have similar concerns. If you're active in the school's parent-teacher organization, you probably know other parents who have similar concerns. If not, ask to speak at the next meeting so that you can express your concerns and ask other parents to join with you.

Since most school board members are elected, having a large group of parents raise concerns—especially if they express them responsibly—can go a long way toward getting the board members to take a second look at the testing policies.

State Policies

Most often, you are likely to find that policies regarding standardized testing are set up at the state level through either a state board of education or legislation. For example, some states have begun to adopt rules about promotion and graduation based on standardized test scores.

Call your local school district and ask who represents your area of the state on the state board of education. Contact that person and ask for an appointment to discuss your concerns. The person may tell you that the state board of education has no control over the policy but that it's a matter of state law. If that's the case, you'll have a much harder battle ahead of you.

Find out who your representative is in the state legislature and arrange a meeting to discuss your concerns, especially if you can take a delegation of parents with similar concerns. Many politicians will welcome the opportunity to meet with concerned voters, especially if the matter is one that they can support. You may not get what you want, but you will at least make the legislator familiar with you and the group you represent.

At this point, if it still doesn't seem that you're going to be able to change anything, contact the National Center for Fair & Open Testing. The Center's Web site (www.fairtest.org) provides a listing of who in your state is coordinating efforts to reform the use of test scores. That person can tell you what resources are available, what other groups are working toward reform, and what legislation or school board policies are under consideration. The Web site also offers links to an array of resources, such as reports, position papers, updates on what is happening in the field of standardized testing, and books that can help you understand the responsible use of standardized tests.

Or contact the local branch of the NAACP. That organization has become particularly sensitive to the misuse of standardized test scores, especially since students who are members of minority ethnic groups frequently bear the brunt of this misuse. Their representatives may have already begun negotiating with the state board of education or the state legislature, and you will be able to add your voice to those of other concerned citizens to fight for change.

Summary

Even if you rationally understand that you should not overreact to your child's group standardized test scores, it is human nature to allow low scores to bother you and make you doubt whether your child is doing well in school. Since children suffer consequences for low test scores in many schools throughout the country, it's important for you to know what your child's scores are and how the schools will use them. If the test scores imply that there is a problem in one or more of your child's academic areas, find out whether there is actually a problem. If you're still in doubt, have your child referred to the child study team at her school.

If you encounter unreasonable policies, you may need to change them. You may have to enlist the help of other concerned parents and join with an advocacy group to work toward responsible use of standardized tests.

If You're a Homeschooler

There was a time in the not-too-distant past when parents who wanted to homeschool their children had to endure endless obstacles. Some faced prosecution for violating school attendance laws. Others faced the scorn and contempt of their neighbors for having the audacity to think they could educate their children better than the schools could.

Today homeschooling is legal in all 50 states. While requirements for the parents' qualifications vary, many states require parents to at least be high school graduates. Many parents find that the motives that led them to consider homeschooling in the first place guide their attitudes toward having their children take state-mandated standardized tests. Some are suspicious toward the assessments and disapprove of the influence standardized tests have come to exert over the public school curriculum.

As one parent put it, "I don't trust those tests. The program my children get at home is so rich that some two-hour test can't tell me whether my children are learning. It doesn't test that we spent last Tuesday at the zoo helping the zookeepers wash the giant turtle. It doesn't test whether my daughter can name every painting in the local university art museum."

On the other hand, some homeschooling parents want their children to have some sort of regular assessment to ensure that they are keeping pace with their peers in basic skill areas. Some of these parents are perfectly willing to have their children go to the local school to take the tests. Others, those who withdrew their children from public school because of safety fears, don't want their children to return to the public school for the tests and may arrange an alternative through homeschooling associations.

State Requirements

Standardized testing requirements for homeschoolers vary tremendously from state to state. Table 5-1 presents testing requirements for each state.

Table 5-1   Standardized Testing Requirements for Homeschoolers*

State	Standardized Tests Required	Comment
Alabama	No	
Alaska	Yes	Grades 4, 6, and 8 [Note 1]
Arizona	No	
Arkansas	Yes	[Note 2]
California	No	

State	Standardized Tests Required	Comment
Colorado	Yes	Grades 3, 5, 7, 9, and 11
Connecticut	No	Portfolio review instead
Delaware	[Note 3]	
District of Columbia	No	
Florida	[Note 4]	
Georgia	Yes	
Hawaii	Yes	Grades 3, 6, 8, and 10
Idaho	No	
Illinois	No	
Indiana	No	
Iowa	[Note 5]	
Kansas	No	
Kentucky	No	
Louisiana	[Note 6]	
Maine	[Note 7]	
Maryland	No	Parents' option
Massachusetts	[Note 8]	
Michigan	No	
Minnesota	Yes	
Mississippi	No	
Missouri	No	
Montana	No	
Nebraska	[Note 9]	
Nevada	Yes	Grades 2, 3, 4, 7, and 8

State	Standardized Tests Required	Comment
New Hampshire	[Note 10]	
New Jersey	No	
New Mexico	Yes	
New York	Yes	Test from approved list
North Carolina	Yes	Must test annually
North Dakota	Yes	
Ohio	[Note 11]	
Oklahoma	No	
Oregon	Yes	Test from approved list
Pennsylvania	Yes	Grades 3, 5, and 8
Rhode Island	[Note 12]	
South Carolina	Yes	
South Dakota	Yes	[Note 13]
Tennessee	Yes	Grades 2, 5, 7, and 9
Texas	No	
Utah	No	
Vermont	[Note 14]	
Virginia	Yes	
Washington	[Note 15]	
West Virginia	Yes	
Wisconsin	No	
Wyoming	No	

Notes

1. Alaska requires students to take standardized tests only if they are enrolled in a full-time, approved correspondence course or a formal program that meets requirements for private or religious schools.

2. Children aged 7 and older are required to take a standardized test from the state's approved list; 14-year-olds must take Arkansas's minimum competency test and provide documentation that they are receiving remediation if they are below standard.

3. The law gives the state education agency the authority to require standardized testing, but the state education agency has not done so.

4. Florida requires evaluation consisting of one or more of the following: standardized testing, portfolio assessment, evaluation by a trained outside party, or any other method approved by the state education agency.

5. Iowa requires either standardized testing, portfolio review, or other approved assessment method.

6. Louisiana requires that homeschooled students take standardized tests or be evaluated by a certified teacher.

7. Maine requires that homeschooled students take standardized tests given by a certified teacher, a local education agency advisory panel, or a homeschool panel that includes a certified teacher.

8. Massachusetts lets local school districts decide whether to require standardized testing of homeschoolers.

9. Nebraska law gives the state board of education the discretion to require standardized testing, but the board currently doesn't require it.

10. Students in New Hampshire must take standardized tests, be evaluated by a certified teacher, or be evaluated using some other approved method.

11. Ohio requires that homeschooled students take standardized tests, be evaluated by a certified teacher, or be evaluated by another approved method.

12. Rhode Island doesn't require statewide standardized testing of homeschooled students, but gives local school districts the authority to require it.

13. In South Dakota, parents may choose to have their homeschooled child evaluated using any nationally standardized test.

14. Homeschooled students in Vermont must take standardized tests or be evaluated by another approved assessment option.

15. Students in Washington must take annual standardized tests or an assessment by a certified person working in education.

Note: These data were accurate when this book went to press. However, homeschooling is a controversial topic in many parts of the country, and the requirements for your area may have changed. *You must contact the director of instruction for your local school district to determine the specific requirements you are required to follow.*

Note that 28 states either require outright that homeschoolers take state-mandated standardized tests or require that parents choose among several alternatives including standardized tests. The most common alternatives to standardized testing include evaluation by a certified teacher, portfolio assessment, or substitution of another test approved by the state. Many homeschooling associations work closely with state departments of public instruction to help parents navigate their way through state-mandated standardized testing requirements.

If Your State Requires Standardized Tests

If you live in one of the states that requires standardized testing of homeschoolers or list it as one of several options, you are very likely to interact with school officials in some capacity.

You probably won't have much contact with state education officials unless you have a grievance against the local school district or you need information or resources that local educators don't have. Most states delegate the task of monitoring homeschoolers to local school districts.

But it's a good idea to know the names of key people in your state department of public instruction that oversee homeschooling and the state's testing program. These individuals can be very helpful, especially if you need information about pending laws, regulations, and interpretations of requirements. Your state's department of public instruction should have a central telephone number. When you call, ask for the department dealing with homeschooling or accountability, and be prepared with specific questions.

Since your school district must keep records of who is being homeschooled, and must enforce any testing provisions, you will probably be dealing more often with local education officials. In fact, usually you must maintain contact with someone (generally an administrator in the district's instruction division) at the local school district to let him or her know that you still live in the district and that you are homeschooling. The person who answers the telephone at the local school district office should be able to refer you to the appropriate person.

It's very important that you establish a good rapport with at least one key person in the school district. Consider that person as your liaison, someone who can answer your questions and help solve problems—or who can refer you to someone who can. The goal is to find someone in the local school district who feels comfortable contacting you and with whom you feel comfortable. Approach this person with the attitude that school personnel aren't the enemy—they are there to help you. You'll find that most school staffers are eager to help you have a good relationship with the school district even though your child no longer attends.

If you live in a state that requires that your homeschooled child take standardized tests, your liaison can tell you what tests your child will be required to take and provide you with the support materials that parents of children who attend the public schools would receive. Your contact person can also help you arrange when and where your child will take the tests.

Many parents simply have their child take the tests with an age-appropriate class and then pick up their child when the tests are finished. If you don't want your child to take the tests with a regular class, your liaison can probably help you arrange for your child to take the tests in a conference room, or to take the tests in a small group during a makeup session.

If you have a problem with the local school district about standardized testing, your liaison can help you learn established procedures for handling grievances. Respect those procedures. The school district administration will certainly respond better to any concerns or grievances you have if you have gone through proper channels. Resist the urge to bypass lower-level administrators and to go directly to the superintendent or school board. It may be time-consuming and frustrating to follow established procedures, but you will get better results if you work your way up the chain of command.

Before you begin a grievance process, make sure you know the laws and regulations on homeschooling. Your school district liaison or your homeschooling association should have these available. Many of the disagreements that homeschooling parents have with school districts concern regulations over which the school districts have no control. If you believe you're being treated unfairly or that the school district is requiring your child to take more tests than the laws require, be sure you have your facts straight. Don't make threats that you can't enforce, and don't make personal attacks against school personnel: Stick to the regulations.

If the disagreement you have is with laws over which the school district has no control, now may be the time to involve other parents who homeschool their children. Talk to parents in your own and other homeschooling associations and determine what advocacy efforts are already under way. Frequently, letter-writing campaigns, public forums, and other avenues for advocating for your position are available to you. If they are not, start them.

If You Want Testing

Even many parents who mistrust group standardized testing want some sort of individual evaluation of how their home-schooled children are doing, just to verify that they are keeping up with their public school peers. These parents have several options, including commercial educational services, certified teachers, licensed school psychologists, and their homeschooling association.

Commercial Educational Services

Several forms of commercial educational services offer standardized testing. The Sylvan Learning Centers and other similar tutorial services offer a range of tests from basic standardized tests to more comprehensive diagnostic tests. Many such centers work with teachers trained to administer individual achievement tests and school psychologists who can provide a full range of intelligence, achievement, and personality tests.

In addition, a growing number of educational consultant services run by educators with advanced degrees cater to both families and school districts. Many of these services can provide educational testing and often work with homeschooling associations to administer the associations' testing programs.

Private schools often offer testing services, even for children who don't attend the school. Check with larger private schools near your home and ask if they offer such services. If they don't, ask who provides theirs.

Teachers

Many teachers have specialized training in achievement testing. Reading specialists, for example, are typically trained to administer individual diagnostic reading tests, just as teachers who teach remedial math are often trained to give individual diagnostic math tests. Special education teachers must test their students regularly and are usually familiar with the full range of individual diagnostic achievement tests. Call your local teacher's college and ask for recommendations. Personnel at your local public school may know of teachers who give these tests as well.

School Psychologists

School psychologists are trained in the full range of educational and psychological testing. These tests are especially helpful if you suspect that your child has some sort of learning problem. In fact, if you suspect that your child has a disability, you can request that the school district in which you live provide a school psychological evaluation at no cost to you.

But be prepared to wait. Even though federal law requires school districts to complete such evaluations within 45 days after a request, most school psychologists who work for the public schools have such large caseloads that it could be months before they can get around to testing your child. They get especially backed up in the last quarter of the school year, so try to make your testing request early in the school year.

The school psychologist can identify a full range of learning disorders and can provide extensive recommendations for treatment. Even if your child doesn't have a learning disorder, the school psychological evaluation can identify his specific learning style to help you teach him. For example, the evaluation might reveal that your child learns better when he can see and feel rather than just see alone. In that case, you would want to include instructional activities that allow him to build models or provide some other type of hands-on activities.

Be prepared to do some searching for a licensed school psychologist in private practice. In many parts of the country, they are in short supply. Look in the telephone book under "Psychologists" and note which ones list a specialty in school psychology. Check with the state psychology licensing board for names of licensed school psychologists in your area. Remember—not all psychologists are school psychologists. Make sure they are trained in that specialty. Check with private schools in your area to see if they have consultant relationships with school psychologists.

Your Homeschooling Association

Many homeschooling associations (especially national associations) offer achievement testing services. But be careful—some of the tests they use might be no more valid for diagnosing individual students' learning than are the group standardized tests that we discuss in the remainder of this book. Be especially wary of brief tests that have a small number of items. Such tests can often provide misleading results.

Ask to speak with a representative of the association who can provide you with additional information on the tests. Ask for brochures. When in doubt, find out what tests the association offers and make an appointment with a school psychologist or educational consultant to discuss whether the tests are appropriate for individual diagnosis.

Summary

Twenty-eight states either require that students who are homeschooled take standardized tests or list standardized tests as one of several testing alternatives. If you live in a state that requires such testing, it's important that you establish a good working relationship with someone at the local school district. Even if your state doesn't require standardized testing, you may want to have your child tested just to make sure she is keeping up with other children. You can arrange such testing through commercial educational services, teachers, school psychologists, or your homeschooling association.

If Your Child Has
Special Needs

Eastern Elementary and Western Elementary are giving the same achievement test to their third graders. The standard directions require that students take the tests in 45-minute sessions over three consecutive school days. The faculty at Eastern follow the standard instructions exactly. But to save time, Western staffers decide to give the entire test in one sitting, lasting slightly more than two hours. Eastern follows instructions to prohibit calculators, but the faculty at Western give calculators to students.

Is it fair to compare the results for the two schools? Of course not. We know what the Eastern students' scores mean because the faculty gave the test in the way the test publisher required—the same way the test was given to the standardization group. But we don't know how to interpret the scores of the Western students because the faculty at that school didn't follow the instructions.

Changing the way we give tests, for whatever reason, weakens the ability to interpret the scores. For this reason, don't be surprised when school authorities aren't eager to make the accommodations you ask for your child, no matter how much you want them made or how fair you think it is to make them. In fact, the school is very likely to resist such changes—and it should, unless you can make a very strong case.

In this chapter, we'll discuss the types of accommodations in group standardized tests that may be necessary as well as the types of students for whom they will be appropriate.

Informal Accommodations

Informal accommodations are reasonable changes teachers make every day in class. For example, they might separate students who misbehave, or close the door to a noisy hall.

Ms. Rollins notes that Timmy and Tabitha spend too much time in class talking, so she decides to separate them during standardized testing.

Mr. Barnes notes that Ben has problems paying attention and tends to stare out the window. When the class takes the Metropolitan Achievement Test, he lowers the shades in the room so that Ben can't look out—and may even move him so he can't hear what's going on outside the building.

Tim is so disruptive in class that his teacher is convinced he'll pose serious disruptions during testing, so she finds an additional proctor for the group to attend mainly to Tim. If Tim's actions interfere with testing for other students even with an extra proctor, it may be necessary to move him to small-group testing.

These accommodations don't require any sort of formal agreements, and teachers usually aren't obligated to get special permission to make them. These accommodations certainly don't detract from test interpretation. In fact, these changes can make the tests more accurate because they remove factors that artificially detract from the validity of the test scores. You might not even be aware that your child's teacher has made these types of accommodations in testing.

But what if parents or teachers propose more extreme accommodations? At one time, schools responded to these requests by simply excluding students whose parents or teachers asked for special changes. In fact, exclusion from testing continues to be a major accommodation that parents and teachers request for students. But because many school districts abused the power to exclude students from testing by using that power as a way to raise district test scores, it's getting harder for schools to exclude all but the most severely handicapped students from testing.

Formal Accommodations

The school may not be so eager to comply when parents or teachers want accommodations that seriously differ from standard directions. For example:

- Charles and Karen Williams ask that their son Michael be allowed to use a calculator on all math sections of standardized tests, even though the test instructions specifically forbid the use of calculators.
- Kelli Jones's teacher asks that Kelli be able to have all test questions read to her although test instructions clearly require that students read the questions themselves.

- Mr. Steele asks that his son be allowed to dictate his answers to all test questions to the teacher even though the test's instructions require students to write out their answers.
- Jason's mother asks to be allowed to be present to keep Jason focused on test questions.
- Ms. Carlisle asks that her son Kevin be able to take the tests in four 22-minute, 30-second periods rather than in the prescribed two 45-minute sessions.

Each of these requests drastically departs from standard directions for how we administer tests. When we make such changes, we don't always know how to interpret students' test scores. Can we interpret math scores the same for two students when one was allowed to use a calculator and the other was not? Can we compare the scores of two other students when an aide read the comprehension passages to one, but the other had to read the passages herself?

Teachers and education administrators can only make such changes with two types of students: those served under the Rehabilitation Act of 1973 and those served under the Individuals with Disabilities Education Act (IDEA).

Rehabilitation Act

Public Law 93-112 (also known as the Rehabilitation Act of 1973) is the law that forces all institutions that get federal money to make their buildings accessible to people with disabilities. It requires ramps, wheelchair-accessible toilets, and modified water fountains. It requires tall buildings to have elevators and Braille markings, and it requires public buses to have wheelchair lifts.

Under the act, a disability is any condition that poses significant limitations to a person's ability to get an education, work, use public transportation, and so on. Disabilities include not only physical disabilities but mental disabilities as well. Disabilities covered under the Rehabilitation Act include:

- A broken arm or leg
- Pregnancy
- Attention deficit hyperactivity disorder (ADHD)
- Depression
- Diabetes
- A seizure disorder
- Tourette's syndrome
- Narcolepsy
- Any physical condition that requires someone to use crutches or a wheelchair
- Bladder disorder requiring clean intermittent catheterization

If a disability interferes with a student's access to testing, the student may qualify for accommodations. And note that a student's disability doesn't have to be permanent to qualify for protection under the Rehabilitation Act. Pregnancy and broken arms, for example, are temporary conditions that limit students' ability to function for a period of time but eventually change. Once these conditions end and the person no longer needs accommodations, the person is no longer covered under the act.

If you think your child needs special accommodations for testing and qualifies under the Rehabilitation Act, contact your school's Child Study Team (see Chapter 4). Team members will gather information about your child's problem and create an Individualized Accommodation Plan (see Figure 6-1).

Figure 6-1   An Example of an Individual Accommodation Plan

Springfield Unified School District
Section 504 Individual Accommodation Plan (IAP)

Name: John Smith   **DOB:** 11/23/1991   **Grade:** 5
School: Springfield Intermediate School   **Meeting Date:** 1/5/2001

1. **Is the student disabled as defined by Section 504 of the Rehabilitation Act of 1973?** Yes

2. **If yes, describe the nature of the concern/disability:** Attention deficit hyperactivity disorder (ADHD)

3. **Describe the basis for the determination of the disability:** Psychological report by Dr. Ross Harris, diagnosis ADHD, primarily inattentive type; medical report by Dr. Stella Legarda, pediatric neurologist, same diagnosis.

4. **Does the disability substantially limit a major life activity?** Yes.

5. **If yes, describe how the disability affects a major life activity:** John is unable to maintain attention and concentration for extended periods. He is particularly distractible and disruptive in group situations.

6. **Describe services/accommodations that are necessary to ensure commensurate opportunity for meeting educational needs:** (1) John will require a dose of 10 mg of Ritalin at 7 a.m. each morning prior to coming to school, followed by 10 mg of Ritalin administered by the school nurse at 11:30 a.m. each day, (2) preferential seating in close proximity to the teacher's desk, (3) daily behavior report card sent home to parents, (4) standardized testing in a separate room under individual supervision of teacher or aide.

As part of the plan, the team members must determine whether the accommodations relate to testing, and if so, how. For example, if your left-handed child broke her left hand, team members might have her try to complete a practice test using her right hand to fill in the answers on the answer sheet. If she can't do this, school personnel would have to figure out how to help her answer the questions in a way that won't differ from standard instructions any more than is necessary. Perhaps your child could take a test in a separate room, calling out answers to an aide, or maybe she could answer the multiple-choice questions on a computer.

Here are some other examples of the types of accommodations that students might receive:

- Rosanne has very poor eyesight but does well in school with special magnifying glasses and large-print materials. She is able to use a large-print version of the standardized test administered in her school.
- Lucas has ADHD. Even though he is taking large doses of medication to help his attention, his teachers must often separate him from other students because they distract each other. He is allowed to take the standardized test in a separate room with an aide administering the tests to him and making sure that he remains focused on the test.
- Amanda takes standardized tests that call for uninterrupted 45-minute sessions. Because Amanda has irritable bowel syndrome, she is allowed to take her standardized tests in a separate room with an adjoining toilet, which she can use whenever necessary during the test. When she goes to the toilet, the aide stops timing. Even though she receives 45 minutes of testing, the actual session may be much longer due to her trips to the toilet.

If Your Request Is Turned Down

First, remember that school personnel must make every reasonable effort to ensure that all students who take group standardized tests take them under conditions that conform to standard instructions. If the school resists your request, the school is probably not trying to give you a hard time. It's up to you to show why the accommodations are appropriate.

First, make sure that the accommodations you request for your child are reasonable. People who work in the schools have had parents come to them requesting all sorts of accommodations, so be prepared for some skepticism on the part of the school. Many parents think they have a right to anything they ask for once their child is identified as eligible for accommodations under the Rehabilitation Act.

Here are some general guidelines to help you decide whether the accommodations you ask for are both reasonable and appropriate:

- *Have an identified disability.* The accommodations should relate to an identified disability. For example, parents may be convinced that their child has ADHD, but no doctor will agree.
- *Be logical.* The accommodations must logically follow from the disability. If your child has a documented problem with frequent urination, he should be allowed to go to the bathroom during testing—but not to have all questions read to him. The fact that your child's vision is so poor that she needs powerful glasses and a magnifying glass doesn't mean she must be allowed to use a calculator on the math sections of the test.
- *Make timely requests.* Make sure you request accommodations as soon as possible. If at the last moment you demand major accommodations, especially if you have not asked for accommodations in your child's daily instruction, the school may suspect that the accommodations may be unnecessary.

If your child has a lifelong disability, make sure you contact the school before she begins school. If your son has a problem such as a broken leg, or you suddenly learn that he has a seizure disorder, bring the matter to the attention of the school as soon as you learn about the problem.

But let's suppose that you have gone through all of the above steps and the school refuses to make the accommodations you request. Yet your child has a documented disability that significantly limits his ability to engage in one or more major life activities, and interferes with his ability to take tests. You've furnished all the necessary documentation for the problem, and you've asked for accommodations that you believe are totally reasonable and appropriate.

Here's what to do next.

***Step 1*. Be persuasive, not combative.**   It's amazing how many parents hire attorneys or enlist the support of advocacy groups without ever expressing their disagreement to school personnel. Often administrators have no idea that parents are unhappy with a Child Study Team decision until the school receives a letter from the parents' attorney.

Make sure to attend every meeting at school about your child. Don't sit home waiting for the Child Study Team to hand down a decision in which you did not participate. Attend the meeting and speak up. Frequently, the very fact that you disagree will be enough to sway members of the team to your way of thinking, especially if you can provide a convincing argument why your request is reasonable.

***Step 2*. Enlist outside help.**   If you have made your objections known and you still can't persuade team members to agree to your accommodation request, you might have to enlist outside help.

When your child comes up before the Child Study Team, you should be given a statement of your rights along with a list of places to go for assistance if you and the team can't agree. The list will usually contain addresses and telephone numbers for advocacy groups who work on behalf of the Office for Civil Rights. If you don't receive such a list or you need further help, you may contact the Office for Civil Rights directly at the U.S. Department of Education, Office for Civil Rights, Customer Service Team, Mary E. Switzer Building, 320 C Street, SW, Washington, DC 20202. Telephone: (800) 421-3481; fax: 202-205-9862; TDD: 877-521-2172; e-mail: OCR@ed.gov.

The Office for Civil Rights can refer you to appropriate advocacy groups in your area where you can obtain legal services. These services are usually free. Staffers at these groups will listen to your concerns and recommend appropriate action. They may tell you that your requests are inappropriate, or they may decide that your child is being wrongfully denied appropriate accommodations and will help you fight for them.

This process usually begins by having the advocacy group or the Office for Civil Rights request a meeting with the person who coordinates services for students served under the Rehabilitation Act for the school district. The advocate will then try to persuade school personnel to agree to the reasonable accommodations.

Sometimes the threat of further action will be enough for you to get what you asked for, especially if there was disagreement among the team members. However, if the school district still does not agree to the accommodations, it may be necessary to file a formal complaint with the Office for Civil

Rights. The Office for Civil Rights would then make a preliminary investigation and may hold a formal hearing. If the school district loses at the hearing, the Office of Civil Rights would direct school personnel to make the requested accommodations under threat of loss of federal funding. If you lose, you will have to decide whether you would prefer to just drop the matter or whether you are willing to go to the time, trouble, and expense of filing a lawsuit.

Individuals with Disabilities Education Act

The Individuals with Disabilities Education Act is the latest revision of Public Law 94-142, which requires school districts to identify students with certain specific handicaps and to provide special education and related services to them. Some of the handicaps served under IDEA include:

- Learning disabilities
- Mental retardation
- Serious emotional disturbance
- Visual or hearing problems
- Orthopedic problems
- Other health problems

You may be confused about the difference between disabilities identified under the Rehabilitation Act and handicaps identified under IDEA. Essentially, the law assumes that students with disabilities identified under the Rehabilitation Act can obtain an appropriate education provided that they receive appropriate accommodations. However, students with handicaps covered under IDEA can't receive an appropriate education without a comprehensive educational program including individualized special education and related services. While the Rehabilitation Act defines a disability as *any* condition that limits an individual's ability to engage in one or more major life activities, IDEA limits handicaps to a set of narrowly defined conditions.

The document that specifies every aspect of the child's educational program under IDEA is the Individualized Education Program, or IEP. The IEP must address whether there will be any changes to testing procedures and what the changes will be.

Until recently, many school districts commonly excluded many students with handicaps from taking standardized tests, whether it was warranted or not, especially if the students had previously scored lower than the school's average on standardized tests. In fact, a widespread practice in many schools until recently was to refer children who scored low on standardized tests for evaluation under IDEA in hopes that the school district could exclude them from taking standardized tests if they could qualify for placement. This practice occurred often enough so that some educators began to demand that the state start checking a school's decisions regarding standardized testing accommodations.

Today it's not so easy to exclude children from standardized testing unless their handicaps are extremely severe. Most state departments of public instruction now require schools to follow fairly strict guidelines on the accommodations they can make. For example, most states now require that students not be excluded from standardized tests unless they function at the very lowest levels of intelligence or their other handicaps are so severe that they can't possibly get an accurate score even with appropriate accommodations.

Students under IDEA are only entitled to testing accommodations that are specifically linked to their specific handicaps. For example:

- Jason has a severe learning disability in reading comprehension, so he can take standardized tests in a separate room where an aide reads test questions to him.
- Marilyn has a learning disability in mathematics calculation, so she is allowed to use a calculator on the mathematics reasoning sections of standardized tests.
- Janet has severe cerebral palsy and is classified as orthopedically handicapped. She can't use her hands to hold a pencil, and her speech is so slow that even when she dictates answers to an aide, she takes much longer to give an answer. Her school decides she can dictate her answers to an aide and can take the tests without being timed.
- George is classified under IDEA with extremely low intelligence that is so poor he isn't very aware of his surroundings. He can't understand most things people say to him, and he can't make his needs known. The school decides his handicap is so severe that he can be excluded from group standardized testing.

If You Disagree

Your rights under IDEA are even broader than with the Rehabiliation Act and, in some instances, bring you greater power to go after what you want for your child.

As the parent of a student served under IDEA, you have the right to be an equal member of the team that determines whether or not your child will be classified as handicapped under IDEA and that constructs the IEP. The IEP must address whether the student has any special needs that relate to testing and what testing accommodations are necessary to meet those needs.

The most important step that you can take as a member of the team is to decide whether testing accommodations are necessary and what they might be. One of the most common unreasonable demands parents make of the schools under IDEA is for testing accommodations that either are unrelated to the child's handicap or are out of proportion to the child's handicap. For example, many parents demand major accommodations such as having the entire test read to a child when the handicap is a mild math calculation problem. Other parents demand that their child be excused from testing altogether even though there is a mild orthopedic handicap that doesn't interfere with normal testing procedures.

You should recognize that school districts can only provide certain accommodations to students, particularly those whose handicaps are relatively mild. If your child has a mild learning disability in basic reading skills but is able to pay attention well and never disrupts the class, it would probably not be appropriate to demand individualized administration of the group standardized tests. If she has a mild hearing handicap but seems to do well in school with a hearing aid and one hour per week special education, then demanding that she be excluded from standardized testing altogether is probably not appropriate.

Start by looking at your child's handicap and at the types of limitations that handicap poses to your child every day. Ask for testing accommodations that are consistent with those limitations and the types of accommodations your child requires. For example, a child who has a learning disability in basic reading skill may provide the incorrect answers to test questions because she misreads them. The math problem may say, "Susie has three brothers," but she may read it as, "Sitting in a tree," or the words may be nonsense to her. In that case, it would be reasonable and appropriate to at least ask that she listen to a tape with the test questions on it or that an aide read the questions to her.

As with parents whose children are served under the Rehabilitation Act, the most effective tool for parents whose children are served under IDEA is a combination of reason and persuasion. Do your homework. Make sure you have read every evaluation your child has ever had and that you are familiar with every special service your child has ever received.

It's important to stay calm when you're trying to persuade members of the Child Study Team to make the accommodations you believe are appropriate. It's only human nature to resent it when someone is threatening or verbally abusive, and school personnel are no exception. If you come into school acting hysterical or making threats that you can't possibly carry out, you'll be labeled an unstable parent and you'll have a much harder time getting cooperation.

But suppose that you've made every effort to explain your child's testing accommodation needs and you're still turned down. You have some rights under IDEA that you wouldn't have under the Rehabilitation Act.

First, you have the right to ask for a local due process hearing. Sometimes just the threat of a hearing will be enough to sway other team members to agree to the accommodation you are seeking. If a hearing is scheduled, you and the school will have an opportunity to speak before an impartial hearing officer. All school districts must maintain lists of individuals qualified to serve as hearing officers. The hearing officer will listen to both sides of the case and then will render a decision.

You're entitled to representation by an attorney, and it's usually worthwhile to have one, especially if you're not sure what your rights are and if you feel overwhelmed or threatened. Make sure your attorney has specific training and experience in special education law. You should receive from the school a list of resources from which you may obtain free or low-cost legal representation as well as a list of the appropriate advocacy groups. You also may contact the Office for Civil Rights.

In many cases, the conflict ends with the decision of the local due process hearing officer. The loser often decides that the chance of getting the decision overturned isn't worth the time, inconvenience, and expense of an appeal. But the loser does have the right to appeal through a state-level due process hearing. If you or the school disagrees with the outcome of the local hearing and wishes to appeal, the hearing officer must notify the state education agency, which will arrange for a state-level hearing.

If you lose at the state level, you can then choose to sue the school district. You would follow the same steps at this point that you would in any other legal action, going as far as the U.S. Supreme Court if necessary.

Something Else to Consider

School districts can't easily change the way they administer group standardized tests. The more they depart from standardized directions, the more reluctant they are to make additional changes and the more evidence they must have to justify those changes. And the more radically the school district departs from standardized test procedures with your child, the less it will be able to defend the test results.

The likelihood that the school district may not be able to include your child's test scores in tallying school, school district, and statewide results may not sound very important. But depending on the particular tests, the number of areas in which there were major departures from standard procedures, and the greater the departure from standard procedures, the more likely it will be that your child's performance will be recorded as a failure regardless of his scores. For example, if your child was allowed to use a calculator during the mathematics reasoning section of the test, not only is it likely that the school district can't report those scores with the other students' scores, but your child's permanent record may reflect a failure on mathematics reasoning.

Summary

School districts must follow directions for administering group standardized tests. No serious accommodations can be made unless your child has an Individualized Accommodation Plan under Section 504 of the Rehabilitation Act or an Individualized Education Program under the Individuals with Disabilities Education Act. The burden is on you to convince the school if you believe your child is entitled to significant accommodations. Neither the Rehabilitation Act nor IDEA gives parents the right to tell schools what to do. If the school refuses to make accommodations you think are justified, you can seek help from advocacy groups, the Office for Civil Rights, and private attorneys.

From California to Iowa

Many school administrators and teachers are quite concerned about standardized test results because their very jobs may depend on producing high test scores. As the public demands accountability, standardized test results have become the primary gauge by which schools are judged.

In the hands of knowledgeable educators and policymakers who know the right way to use standardized test results, scores can be a valuable tool in evaluating groups of students and determining whether tax dollars are being used appropriately. But there are some rules that must be followed. In this chapter, we'll discuss some of the principles behind the appropriate use of standardized tests and provide some examples of the right and wrong ways to use standardized tests.

Testing experts rely on a set of authoritative standards for testing called *Standards for Educational and Psychological Testing,* published jointly by the American Educational Research Association, the American Psychological Association, and the National Council on Measurement in Education. The *Standards* provide the basis for how educational and psychological tests are constructed, how they are administered, and how results should be used. If there is a court challenge about standardized tests, the courts base their decision on the *Standards*.

The most important point in the *Standards* emphasizes that tests must be used as they were designed to be used, to measure only what they were designed to measure. Before people use an educational or psychological test to make important decisions, they must be able to produce evidence that they are using the tests appropriately.

So let's look at how to use standardized tests with groups and with individuals.

Group Tests

The most important thing to remember is that group tests assess *groups,* not individuals. Group standardized tests can be used to test many students quickly and efficiently. Educators and legislators see a need to compare large groups of students to identify where students are doing well and where there are problems. It would be difficult and expensive to test large groups of students individually.

Even if there were enough school psychologists to test every child in every school district every year, and even if it were appropriate to repeat the same individual psychological tests year after year, the public wouldn't put up with the extra expense. But there is a much cheaper alternative.

The major test companies have constructed group standardized tests that, for only dollars per child, can quickly test as many children as necessary. Since only minimal training is required for the person actually handing out and monitoring the test (to make sure that the test takes place under standard conditions and the students follow standard instructions), it's an easy matter to test all children at the same time.

For the most part, children taking standardized tests answer multiple-choice questions on special scanning sheets. (See Chapter 2 for more information on multiple-choice questions.) With multiple-choice tests, we can more readily agree on the correct answer.

But sometimes there can be problems even with objective scoring, including mistaken scoring, limitations on what can be tested, and superficiality.

Mistakes

Did you ever receive an incorrect phone bill or perhaps a credit card charge for something you never bought? Computer programs contain errors, the equipment breaks down, scanners don't scan, people enter incorrect information, and so on. With standardized tests, sometimes test developers give programmers erroneous answer keys or the programmers key in the wrong answers. At other times, students make stray marks on their test forms that cause the computers to scan improperly.

You might remember, for example, when a testing company's mistake sent nearly 9000 New York City students to summer school or caused them to repeat a grade. A similar error by the same company nearly sent another 5000 South Carolina students to summer school by mistake. These problems in both New York City and South Carolina highlight the fact that parents can't afford to accept the results of so-called objective scoring.

Limits

Another problem with objectively scored questions is the limits they place on what can be tested. The multiple-choice format can only ask questions that a student answers by choosing among alternatives. The questions must be written so students can recognize the correct answers. But what about the ability to build an argument for one position or another and to justify that position? What about the ability to describe the plot of a novel? It's almost impossible to assess this greater depth of knowledge using multiple-choice questions.

Superficiality

It's impossible to fairly test every aspect of every curriculum. It's more efficient and cost-effective to develop tests that represent the general subjects most children study in school. As long as we use large numbers of students to make comparisons, it's usually possible to make some reasonably valid comparisons among large groups.

For instance, we assume that most children learn the difference between a noun and a verb; that they learn addition, subtraction, multiplication, and division; and that they read some classic novels such as *The Red Badge of Courage* or *Little Women* during their school careers. So test companies construct standardized test items that test students' learning in a broad way. This represents a trade-off between cost-effectiveness and the degree of emphasis we can put on the scores since the scores don't reflect the many layers of learning that are taking place.

For example, the test scores may provide a good way to determine how fifth grade students at Clark Intermediate School are learning general language arts concepts, but they don't take into account the fact that the school administration decided to put a strong emphasis on writing and that three of the fifth grade students won first places in national writing competitions this year.

At Sam Houston Elementary School, the test scores reveal that many of the students aren't proficient in basic language arts when tested in English. They don't tell us that 60 percent of the students use English as a second language but that the school has a very strong English as a second language curriculum that is making a tremendous impact on students' ability to learn English.

To make up for the superficiality of the information that standardized tests provide in comparing groups of students, it's necessary to take into account other factors when evaluating groups of students, such as:

- How comparable are the groups in ethnic and income characteristics? How many students in each group receive free lunch? Are there about the same proportions of different races?
- What are the educational backgrounds of the parents? Are we comparing students in one group who come from homes in which neither parent finished high school against students with college-educated parents?
- Do the groups have similar available resources? Does one group have new computer labs with the latest educational software and a well-stocked library with up-to-date

resources, but the other comes from schools in poor communities with no computers, a poor library, and outdated multimedia resources?

Right Way to Use Standardized Tests

Group standardized tests can be used effectively to compare one grade with another or one school with another, or to determine change over time.

Dr. Elwine, the principal at Eagle Lake Elementary School, suspects that the fourth grade math curriculum at her school is weak. Since students in grades 1 through 5 take the Stanford Achievement Test every year, she pulls out the latest standardized test math scores and plots the average scores on a piece of graph paper. She sees that the scores in grades 1, 2, and 3 are usually at about the same level but that they drop in fourth grade and then slowly rise in fifth grade. She decides there is good reason to look deeper into the possibility that there is a problem with the fourth grade math curriculum.

Meanwhile, the school board of Fairfield School District wants to know how its students at West Gate Middle School are learning compared with students in other middle schools in the area. The board finds several other area schools with the same educational and economic levels, similar racial and ethnic makeup, and equivalent level of faculty education. The school board compares the TerraNova scores of West Gate Middle School with those of the other schools and finds that West Gate students scored slightly higher in math but slightly lower in language arts than the other schools.

Jim Hicks came to Dove Elementary School as principal three years ago. Dove is located in what had been a thriving community until a major plant shut down, leaving most parents unemployed and their families on food stamps. Those who didn't move away to find other jobs were mainly uneducated, chronically unemployed parents. Currently, 92 percent of the children at the school are on free lunch, and parent attendance at the parent-teacher meetings has been so poor that the organization stopped meeting four years ago.

Mr. Hicks knows that the school's Iowa Tests of Basic Skills scores have been the lowest in the county for the past five years, but he aggressively recruits strong teachers with solid reputations and badgers the school district administration for books, computers, building repairs, and money for field trips.

Although the school's test scores are still the lowest in the county, Mr. Hicks proudly shows the school board a chart depicting strong growth in the school's test scores over the past three years, with a significant decrease in student and faculty absenteeism and resurrection of the school's parent-teacher organization.

Wrong Ways to Use Group Standardized Test Scores

Many of the most blatant misuses of standardized tests with groups come from the mistaken level of faith many lawmakers and even educators (who should know better) place in standardized test scores. They will frequently consider test scores as the only indicator of how groups of students are learning.

For example, King Elementary School serves the poorest community in the school district, with the highest crime and truancy rates and parents with the least education. Even though the school continues to have the lowest standardized test scores of any school in the district, there have been tremendous improvements in test scores since Dr. Damson was hired as principal. School attendance and teacher morale have improved.

But the school board warns Dr. Damson that if the school's test scores remain below the national average, she will lose her job. The local paper runs a feature about the school's low test scores. Sadly, the school board and the newspaper ignore how students' learning is affected by the community's poverty and the poor educational level of the parents—and that ultimately, this affects standardized test scores.

On the other hand, Northern Elementary is situated in the most affluent part of the county, and most of its students come from homes in which both parents completed college. The school is situated close to the headquarters for Acme Industries, and the children of many of the highly paid top executives at Acme attend the school. Acme has built state-of-the-art multimedia and computer labs at the school and donates thousands of dollars a year for library books and other programs.

Each year, the principal takes credit for the school's ranking of highest test scores in the county. The principal and the school board credit the high scores in the school to their leadership and innovative educational practices.

The America's Finest program's charter says that its mission is to identify the best schools in the country. Each year, schools from all over the country apply for the America's Finest designation. The main yardstick the program uses to compare the schools is scores from group standardized tests. It ignores improvements in test scores over time and could not care less about factors such as the racial and ethnic composition and the economic and educational levels of the families the students come from. Invariably, the program identifies schools from affluent, predominately white, suburbs as America's Finest.

The test publishers for the large, commercially prepared group standardized tests (such as those discussed in Chapters 8 through 12) are able to produce research findings that their tests can tell how students in large groups as a whole are mastering basic academic skills. Comparing large groups of students on broad areas measured by group standardized tests generally meets the criteria set forth in the *Standards.*

Not a Diagnostic Tool

One of the first lessons that new graduate students in psychology learn is that no single test can tell us everything we need to know about anyone. Remember that to make it possible to test large groups of students quickly, efficiently, and cheaply, and to make it possible for people with very little training to administer group standardized tests in a standard manner, we have to make some sacrifices.

Since standardized tests generate information on individual students, administrators find it very tempting to use those results to diagnose individual students' learning. But there are many reasons why this is inappropriate.

To be able to machine-score large numbers of test sheets, test questions must be multiple-choice or true/false. Questions also must be broad so they can focus on general aspects of most curricula. Finally, these tests usually make conclusions about broad academic areas on the basis of only several dozen multiple-choice items, and therefore, there is just not enough information from them to provide definitive diagnoses for individual students. Table 7-1 summarizes some similarities and differences between individual psychological tests and group standardized tests.

Table 7-1   A Comparison of Individual Psychological Tests and Group Standardized Tests

	Individual Psychological Tests	Group Standardized Tests
Content	Specific: Some, in fact, can be very specific	General: Some, in fact, can be quite superficial
Cost per individual	Relatively expensive	Relatively inexpensive
Time required	Relatively lengthy administration	Relatively quick administration
How many students we can test in one sitting	One	As many as we want
Examiner qualifications	Professional, multi-year degree (such as psychologist or speech and language therapist) required	Briefing regarding standard administration procedures, usually through reading a pamphlet or attending an in-service workshop
How flexible are procedures	Moderately rigid: The person administering the test must follow standard directions, but there is some provision for alteration of procedures under prespecified conditions	Extremely rigid: The person administering the test must ensure that only designated procedures are followed
How valuable the test is for diagnosis of individual learning	High value as one point of data	Moderately poor value even as one point of screening data; must be supplemented by extensive additional information

	Individual Psychological Tests	Group Standardized Tests
Starting and ending point determination	Usually determined individually: Work backward until the student correctly answers a certain number of questions in a row and then work forward until the student misses a certain number of questions in a row	Everyone taking the same test begins and ends at the same place
Provision for year-after-year administration	Typically designed to be administered once or only a few subsequent times, with intervals between testing of six months to three years minimum	Due to the presence of alternate forms, it is possible to administer yearly

Another problem with making individual assessments based on group standardized tests involves the qualifications of the examiner. Before psychologists may administer individual intelligence or achievement tests, they must take many advanced classes in test theory, learning, and statistics. They must study various learning disorders, review hundreds of case files, and administer and report the results of hundreds of tests under supervision. When psychologists conduct an individual examination of a student's knowledge, they know in detail what information the test scores reveal. But they are also trained to be sensitive to any factors that may make a child respond in an unreliable manner, such as illness, emotional upset resulting from, say, a death in the family, uncomfortable testing environment, vision or hearing problems, and so on.

The person administering group tests, in contrast, does not have the training to be attentive to the kinds of problems that might cause students' test scores to be unreliable. Unless children come up and insist that they are too sick to continue, the examiner isn't in a position to determine that testing should be discontinued. And since the test company, not the person giving the test, provides the score report, there is no way for the person giving the test to provide any insight about whether the results are reliable.

This doesn't mean that the group standardized score reports that come home with your child are useless. They provide one bit of information—but *not* the whole picture. Think of the health screenings you've probably seen at your local shopping mall. The health fair booths offer shoppers screenings of a range of health issues, such as:

- Vision
- Hearing
- Weight
- Blood pressure
- Cholesterol
- Blood sugar level
- Spinal straightness
- Posture

Sam Smith, a 67-year-old retired truck driver, goes to the health fair and learns that his blood pressure is high and his vision is not as good as it might be. The nurse performing the vision screening also notes that it looks as if Sam may have a cataract in the right eye. There's no doctor standing there to issue Sam a prescription for blood pressure medication or to arrange for him to see an ophthalmologist to have the cataract evaluated or removed. These are only screenings, and so the nurse advises Sam to make appointments with his doctor and his eye care professional to discuss the results.

In the same way that we use these screenings at a health fair to determine if we have a health problem that may warrant a visit to the doctor, you can use the results of group standardized tests as one point of information to help spot a learning problem and to indicate the need for further individual testing.

For example, Sammy is doing well in school. He completes his assignments and makes good grades. His math calculation score on the group standardized test from last spring was below average, but his teachers look over his math work and don't see a problem. They decide to monitor him for problems but not to take the low group standardized test score very seriously.

Melissa, however, isn't doing well in school. Her class work and test grades are below average. She's already repeating third grade, and it doesn't look as if she will be promoted to fourth. Her teacher and parents have accumulated a portfolio of her work that shows that she doesn't understand even basic skills in any of her subjects. Everyone agrees that she tries very hard. Her group standardized test scores were so low that several sections were unscorable.

Her parents note that she often seems very frustrated at homework time, and she'll cry and fuss to avoid doing it. They decide to refer her to the Child Study Team at her school to determine whether the school psychologist should evaluate her for a handicap.

Unfortunately, schools too often use group standardized results with individuals in ways that aren't appropriate. For example, Leslie is doing well in fourth grade and making top grades in each subject. She seems happy in school, and everyone agrees that she's an eager, effective student. But her group standardized test results indicated that her math is below average, and so Leslie is placed in the school's compensatory math program. She must leave her class each day so she can receive math instruction at a much lower level. The test publisher is unable to provide any research evidence that the test actually distinguishes between individual students who are and aren't learning math effectively. In fact, the publisher provides a cautionary statement in its test manual that it's not valid for interpretation with individual students. In this case, the school district's use of the test results as the sole criterion to place students into compensatory math does not meet the criteria provided in the *Standards*.

Jared's group aptitude test score was very high, as were all his scores on the group standardized test. Because of these scores, he is placed into the school's gifted program. Sarah had average scores on the group aptitude test and only slightly above average scores on the group achievement test, which disqualify her from participation in the school's gifted program. Yet there is no evidence, either from the publisher or from any other source, that the particular standardized test can discriminate between gifted and nongifted students. This use of the group standardized test scores violates the requirement expressed in the *Standards* that those who use test results must provide convincing evidence that the test is being used in a valid manner.

In South Carolina, students who don't qualify for placement in their schools' gifted programs no longer have the option of going outside the school district to obtain private individual testing. Recent regulations by the state board of education specifically prohibit schools from substituting private, individual intelligence testing—even with individually administered instruments that were actually designed to discriminate between gifted and nongifted students and given by properly trained and licensed school psychologists—for group standardized test results in classifying children as gifted. There is a substantial body of research that the Stanford-Binet Intelligence Scale the private psychologists use does discriminate between students who are and who aren't gifted. The use of the individually administered Stanford-Binet Intelligence Scale meets the criteria specified by the *Standards,* but the regulations prohibit parents from obtaining those results from private psychologists.

Rather, parents are forced to follow the results of the group standardized tests, although there is no evidence that they can discriminate between students who are and who aren't gifted. The use of the group standardized tests for placement of students in South Carolina as gifted would not meet requirements set forth in the *Standards.*

Summary

Group standardized test results are best used to compare groups of students. We should be extremely cautious when using group standardized test scores with individuals for many reasons, since the tests were never designed to provide detailed diagnostic information for single students. These tests can be useful as one bit of information in discovering students who need further assessment, but learning problems or giftedness should never be diagnosed in individual students on the basis of scores from group standardized aptitude or achievement tests.

The TerraNova Series: The Comprehensive Test of Basic Skills and the California Achievement Test

The TerraNova series is a comprehensive group of standardized tests published by CTB/McGraw-Hill, which has offered a wide range of tests and services for more than 70 years. The publisher currently helps school districts administer and score more than 20 million tests a year, and furnishes 23 state education departments with major testing products.

With the recent addition of the latest revision of the California Achievement Test, the publisher now offers two versions: the TerraNova CTBS, featuring the Comprehensive Test of Basic Skills (CTBS), and the TerraNova CAT, featuring the California Achievement Test (CAT).

The CTBS and the CAT have long been mainstays of standardized testing in the United States. The two versions of the TerraNova measure the same skill areas and may be considered alternate forms.

Features of the TerraNova

With both versions, the TerraNova development team studied input from teachers, school administrators, students, and parents to determine what would make the test more user-friendly than previous standardized tests. As a result, the new versions have richer graphics, with the look and feel of the sort of materials that students encounter in school every day. Artwork, page layout, and color were chosen to capture students' interest.

TerraNova developers also wanted to create tests that correspond to students' daily experience. New illustrations, graphics, and photographs were designed to match those that students would encounter every day in magazines and books, with up-to-date stories and art.

Then, during the design phase of the TerraNova, experts observed children taking the tests to assess how user-friendly the materials were. Were they easy to read? Was it easy for the students to move from one page or section to the next? Were the graphics effective? The developers also conducted blind focus groups of veteran teachers and school administrators and asked them to provide detailed opinions and feedback regarding specific elements and the design of the tests.

Decision-Making Tools

The two versions of the TerraNova feature revised interpretation guides for parents and teachers that help them better understand the tests and how they relate to the typical classroom curriculum. Their *Classroom Connections* materials provide teacher aids for instruction planning, and the publisher claims that they help educators make better decisions.

State departments of public instruction and local school districts can receive expanded reports of results, and have the option of receiving data on CD-ROM to help them archive and retrieve data and generate a wide range of reports. The TerraNova reports of test results are so comprehensive that they were used in Chapter 3 as a model for interpretation of score reports.

According to the publisher, having the same skill areas on the TerraNova CAT as the TerraNova CTBS allows for easy comparison of results from the two versions. However, since the two versions feature different tests, parents and school administrators should be very cautious about overinterpretation of differences between scores on the two versions since they are, in effect, comparing apples and oranges.

The TerraNova comes in several modular versions to allow state departments of public instruction and local school districts to purchase only the materials they need. The "Contents" section later in this chapter describes the different options in detail.

Bias Reduction

Standardized tests have historically been notorious for being biased against certain ethnic and cultural groups. In the past, critics of standardized tests have noted that publishers chose the content of some standardized tests from the white, middle-class segment of society. Minority groups, especially Native American, African-American, and Hispanic students, were not familiar with the content, and as a possible result, they made lower scores.

The publisher claims that it has made every attempt to ensure that the content of the two current versions is as unbiased as possible by closely examining bias-reduction studies and using what they learned to help them include more culture-free content or content that would be familiar to cultures other than the white middle class. Throughout the test-writing procedure, the publisher followed the belief that the best way to guard against bias was to develop test questions that actually measure what the questions claim to measure fairly and accurately.

The CTB/McGraw-Hill development team also used the *McGraw-Hill Guidelines for Bias-Free Publishing,* which the company developed to help eliminate bias. The team issued specific guidelines to test makers to help them avoid bias or cultural and gender stereotyping. An internal review team then carefully examined each test item to make sure that it met those guidelines.

The publisher also asked educational professionals representing various ethnic groups to examine all test materials to determine whether the test questions met the guidelines for appropriate language, subject matter, and representation. In addition, CTB/McGraw-Hill conducted sophisticated statistical analyses to discover any statistical biases in test items by carefully examining whether there was any relationship between students' ethnic groups and their test scores.

Test Validity

The TerraNova development team examined the curricula, textbooks, and standards used in different states. They also met with education experts to help construct test items that matched the information students encounter in their schools. The development team conducted many studies to compare students' TerraNova scores with their scores on other standardized tests, and found that the TerraNova does compare very strongly with other similar tests.

Contents

The two versions of the TerraNova assess the same subject areas. School districts or state education agencies are able to buy just the components they need and not those they won't administer.

TerraNova: Complete Battery

The Complete Battery contains the full versions of each of the tests offered on all the TerraNova versions. The Complete Battery has two parts, the core tests and the supplemental tests.

The core tests include:

- Reading/Language Arts
- Mathematics
- Science
- Social Studies

The supplemental tests include:

- Word Analysis
- Vocabulary
- Language Mechanics
- Spelling
- Mathematics Computation

Multiple Assessments

The Multiple Assessments module measures important basic and applied skills. It includes not only multiple-choice questions but also short-answer and essay questions. The publisher scores the multiple-choice answers by machine, but hires professional staff who have been specifically and extensively trained in scoring essays in a reliable and consistent manner.

The Multiple Assessments module emphasizes core subjects that allow comparison of school, school district, and state results to the areas commonly assessed by other tests in other states. Specific tests in this module include:

- Reading/Language Arts
- Mathematics
- Science
- Social Studies

TerraNova: Survey

CTB/McGraw-Hill created the Survey module for those situations in which time is a prime consideration and norm-referenced scores are needed without the depth or full range of reports available on the Complete Battery. It emphasizes a broad assessment of the academic areas covered on the Complete Battery, but in a much shorter time.

In addition to norm-referenced information, the Survey module provides information to assist school personnel in correlating the results to curricula. As with the Complete Battery, the Survey module offers core and supplemental tests:

Core Tests
• Reading/Language Arts
• Mathematics
• Science
• Social Studies

Supplemental Tests (Survey Plus)
• Word Analysis
• Vocabulary
• Language Mechanics
• Spelling
• Mathematics Computation

TerraNova: Custom Modules

CTB/McGraw-Hill also works with school districts to provide other combinations of the above assessments as needed. The typical schools that require custom modules are those with unique curriculum objectives not measured by the other available tests.

CTB/McGraw-Hill can provide supplemental test items designed to measure these unique objectives. The publisher has tried to match the TerraNova objectives to the curricula in many states. The custom modules provide additional assessments for areas not typically assessed.

9

The Iowa Tests of Basic Skills

The Iowa Tests of Basic Skills (ITBS) has been a popular student assessment tool for more than 60 years. Riverside Publishing Company marketed the newest version of the ITBS (Form M) in 1995. University of Iowa test authors revised the ITBS to include the newest and most current test items.

Features at a Glance

According to the publisher, the ITBS Form M has the following new or enhanced features:

- Enhanced graphics. The familiar format of teaching materials that students encounter every day.
- Score reports. Attractive, informative reports for teachers, counselors, administrators, and parents. Riverside now

makes available a new report that tracks students' scores as the students progress from grade to grade.

- A supplement with short-answer and essay questions that allow students to demonstrate deeper knowledge of subject matter.
- Extended performance assessments.
- Separate writing and listening assessments.
- A new, optional, student questionnaire that allows consideration of nonscore data.
- Bias protection. The publisher tried to reduce gender, ethnic, and cultural bias by submitting all items to panels of experts representing these groups and eliminating or modifying items those experts believed were biased.
- Consistent grade-based standards and content standards determined by a national panel of curriculum experts.

The ITBS, Form M

Form M offers two primary sets of tests: The Complete Battery and the Survey Battery. The Complete Battery provides many questions that assess broad academic areas, including:

- Reading
- Language Arts
- Mathematics
- Social Studies
- Science
- Information Sources

The Survey Battery offers assessments of the same broad academic areas as the Complete Battery but in less depth, for those situations in which quicker results are needed.

Form M's Sources of Information test is unique to the ITBS. This assessment measures students' abilities to locate information and interpret and evaluate information sources, and it tests a student's ability to use standard information sources such as dictionaries, encyclopedias, maps, and globes.

The format of Form M provides several enhancements over previous editions. The tests for kindergarten through third grade include expanded items with a more open and appealing format in an attempt to hold a young child's attention. The current edition also includes more black-and-white and color graphics.

The development team carefully considered the recommendations of teachers and curriculum experts to provide artwork and a format similar to the instructional materials that students encounter in school every day. However, the development team also took care to ensure that the expanded graphics and user-friendly look and feel of the scales don't detract from the accuracy of the scales.

Recommended Levels

Form M includes 14 levels across grade levels and curriculum areas.

Kindergarten and Grade 1 (Levels 5 and 6). Levels 5 and 6 are untimed to prevent the frustration that younger students sometimes experience with timed tests. Due to the limited reading ability of young students, all tests except Level 6 reading are administered orally.

Test response forms at these levels also take into account a young child's problems in navigating through a test by allowing students to mark their responses next to the answer choices. The test booklets have bright, open pages with large picture responses, using simple line drawings of animals and everyday objects to help young students find correct test pages.

The Complete Battery for Levels 5 and 6 includes the following tests:

- Vocabulary
- Listening
- Language
- Mathematics
- Word Analysis (optional)
- Reading (optional)

Grades 1, 2, and 3 (Levels 7 and 8). Levels 7 and 8 offer three sets of tests, including a Complete Battery, a Core Battery, and a Survey Battery. The Complete Battery provides these tests:

- Vocabulary
- Reading
- Listening
- Mathematics Concepts
- Mathematics Problems
- Social Studies
- Science
- Sources of Information
- Word Analysis (optional)
- Mathematics Computation (optional)

The Core Battery provides the same assessment as the Complete Battery but without Social Studies, Science, and Sources of Information.

The Survey Battery provides selected items from:

- Vocabulary
- Reading
- Language
- Mathematics Concepts
- Mathematics Problems
- Mathematics Computation (optional)

Grades 3-9 (Levels 9-14). Riverside offers a Complete Battery and a Core Battery. Tests in the Complete Battery include:

- Reading
- Language
- Mathematics
- Social Studies
- Science
- Sources of Information

The Core Battery also includes a choice of separate editions of a four-part language test or a single, integrated writing test.

The development team for levels 9–14 made a special effort to make test booklet pages more attractive and interesting, with photographs, art, graphics, and the look and feel of instructional materials. Test booklets for this level are available as either reusable or machine-scorable booklets.

Optional Assessments

Riverside offers additional, optional assessments to allow school districts more flexibility in designing their testing programs.

The Student Questionnaire consists of 17 items asking students about their educational history, reading and study habits, use of free time, and use of resources such as computers and libraries.

The Constructed Supplement to the Iowa Tests provides open-ended questions on reading, language, and mathematics tests, for which students provide short answers or essay answers.

The Performance Assessments for the ITBS requires students to demonstrate strategic thinking and problem-solving abilities. It provides assessments on integrated language arts, mathematics, social studies, and science.

The Iowa Writing Assessments for the ITBS tests writing skills in narrative, descriptive, persuasive, and expository types of writing. It complements the ITBS language tests by assessing a student's ability to generate, organize, and express ideas.

The Listening Assessment for ITBS provides a wide variety of listening tasks ranging from immediate recall of events or details to higher-level listening skills. The main skills tested include literal meaning, inferential meaning, following directions, visual relationships, and numerical, spatial, and temporal relationships. Students must demonstrate an ability to discern the speaker's purpose, point of view, and style.

Metropolitan Achievement Tests

The Metropolitan Achievement Tests, Eighth Edition (METROPOLITAN8), is the current revision of the Metropolitan Achievement Tests published by Harcourt Educational Measurement.

Its current revision is the product of many years' effort to construct a standardized group achievement test that is both user-friendly and accurate, according to the publisher. The development team thoroughly reviewed kindergarten through twelfth grade textbooks and curricula to determine the content and format of test items appropriate for students at each level.

The team collaborated with education curriculum experts and thoroughly reviewed research on group standardized achievement tests to match content to what is typically provided to students. The team reviewed every item on every test for content, style, appropriateness, and bias. It developed the tests appropriate for a broad range of students, including students with special needs. The team made great effort to eliminate ethnic, cultural, racial, and gender bias.

METROPOLITAN8 Features

Harcourt Educational Measurement emphasizes the following general features of this new revision:

- Flexible assessment times that give schools more options to make changes in the way tests are given. This flexibility is especially important for early grades where young students often become very frustrated with long tests.
- New user-friendly design and ease of use for a student-friendly, up-to-date look like the instructional materials that students encounter every day.
- More information in score reports for teachers and parents.
- Shorter tests that increase students' focus and attention.
- Alternative versions (including Braille, large print, and audiotaped editions) for students with special needs.
- Open-ended assessments in reading, mathematics, and writing.
- Customized assessments that allow for multiple options, such as deciding which tests to include, choosing the test order, and including the OLSAT7 (an aptitude test described in Chapter 11) in students' test booklets. The SelectPlus service allows more customization options, including adding or deleting questions or incorporating locally designed questions into tests.
- Thirteen test levels based on grade are described in Table 10-1.

Table 10-1 Metropolitan Achievement Tests, Eighth Edition, Levels

Grade Range	METROPOLITAN8 Level
Kg.0–Kg.5	PP
Kg.5–1.5	PR
1.5–2.5	P1
2.5–3.5	P2
3.5–4.5	E1
4.5–5.5	E2
5.5–6.5	I1
6.5–7.5	I2
7.5–8.5	I3
8.5–9.5	I4
9	S1
10	S2
11–12	S3

METROPOLITAN8 Content

The METROPOLITAN8 provides tests for the same general areas as the other major group standardized tests, using both multiple-choice and open-ended items. Table 10-2 shows the broad areas tested and whether the items are multiple choice or open-ended.

Table 10-2 METROPOLITAN8 General Academic Area Tests

Area	Multiple-Choice Items	Open-Ended Items
Reading	X	X
Mathematics	X	X
Language	X	
Writing		X
Science	X	
Social Studies	X	

Depending on the test level, there are various skills tested under each subject. Table 10-3 provides information
regarding the specific academic areas tested at each level.

Table 10-3   Specific Subject Areas Tested by Test Level

Test/Level	PP	PR	P1	P2	E1	E2	I1	I2	I3	I4	S1	S2	S3
Sounds and Print	X	X	X	X	X								
Reading Vocabulary			X	X	X	X	X	X	X	X	X	X	X
Reading Comprehension			X	X	X	X	X	X	X	X	X	X	X
Sounds and Print/ Total Reading	X	X	X	X	X	X	X	X	X	X	X	X	X
Mathematics	X	X									X	X	X
Mathematics Concepts and Problem Solving			X	X	X	X	X	X	X	X			
Mathematics Computation			X	X	X	X	X	X	X	X			
Total Mathematics	X	X	X	X	X	X	X	X	X	X	X	X	X
Language	X	X	X	X	X	X	X	X	X	X	X	X	X
Spelling			X	X	X	X	X	X	X	X	X	X	X
Science			X	X	X	X	X	X	X	X	X	X	X
Social Studies			X	X	X	X	X	X	X	X	X	X	X

METROPOLITAN8 Reports

A comprehensive set of reports is provided with each score.
These reports include specific actions to help teachers,
administrators, and parents plan instructional activities. The
score reports provide students' performance levels. They
also include supplemental information about the scores that

reflect thinking and research skills, among others. The publisher also provides score reports matching students' performance on METROPOLITAN8 subject areas with state and local performance standards.

Harcourt Educational Measurement also offers a unique Lexile Student Pathfinder Report that claims to match student reading levels to reading materials. This report also provides a list of literature titles appropriate for the student's reading level.

CHAPTER

Stanford Achievement Test

The Stanford Achievement Test became the nation's first achievement test in 1923. Although crude in comparison with today's standardized tests, the original test was the first step in a movement to objectively measure how well students are learning in school.

Harcourt Brace markets the modern version of the Stanford Achievement Test Series—the Ninth Edition. (This test is frequently referred to in the schools as the STAN9, SAT9, or Stanford9. To avoid confusion with the Scholastic Achievement Test, we will refer to it as the Stanford9.)

General Features

The Stanford9 development team made a strong effort to increase the scale's emphasis on thinking skills. Improved areas of strength include:

- *Multiple-Choice Items.* Harcourt Brace advertises that the Stanford9 has greatly enhanced items drawn from real-life situations. Many items measure strategies and processes.
- *Open-Ended Items.* States and school districts have the option to use open-ended items (such as essay questions) separately, or as an add-on to complement multiple-choice assessments. The scoring system Harcourt Brace uses to grade students' open-ended items allows partial credit as opposed to the all-or-nothing scoring for multiple-choice tests.
- *Reading, Listening, and Writing Items.* These assess skills in a realistic manner with subjects drawn from real life. The company commissioned published children's authors and illustrators to provide reading passages and illustrations unique to the Stanford9.
- *Mathematics Items.* Math abilities are assessed with an emphasis on the ability to understand and apply common mathematical principles. The items involve subjects with which students will be familiar and comfortable.
- *Science and Social Science Items.* These types of questions emphasize the mastery of these two subject areas.

How the Test Looks

The Stanford9 comes in many varieties, including full-length, abbreviated, and open-ended batteries ranging from kindergarten to a year after twelfth grade. Harcourt Brace also offers a variety of customization options, including the opportunity to add state determined or locally determined items.

Schools also can include the aptitude test Otis-Lennon School Abilities Test, Seventh Edition (OLSAT7), with the achievement tests. Using the aptitude projections from the

OLSAT7, school personnel can determine students' predicted achievement levels and can then compare the predicted with the actual achievement to identify potential learning problems. (See Chapter 12 for descriptions of aptitude tests and their uses.)

Fairness

As all other test publishers, Harcourt Brace was also concerned with eliminating test bias. One common source of test bias lies in directions that students receive. To minimize or eliminate test bias from this source, the development team emphasized clear, simple instructions that would be understandable to students of various ethnic, racial, and socioeconomic groups.

One problem test administrators noted in the past was the frequency with which they had to stop test sessions to clarify directions. Many students found it difficult to maintain concentration with all the starts and stops. To combat this problem, students receive a complete set of instructions at the beginning of each test sitting.

Test Format and Page Layout

The development team tried to design page layouts for the test booklets that were easy to use. In the past, many students with little exposure to age-appropriate learning materials outside of class found it hard to go from one section of the page to the next or from one page to the next.

The current version also includes a hard-easy format. In this format, easy questions surround difficult questions in an effort to maintain student interest and avoid the tendency to give up that students have shown in the past when repeatedly confronted with clumps of difficult items.

General Bias

To further guard against test bias, the development team submitted all test items to panels of educators drawn from minority groups to judge the appropriateness of questions, and conducted extensive statistical studies to eliminate items that displayed a statistical bias in favor of or against specific groups.

Stanford9 Content

The Stanford9 is consistent with the current state of educational knowledge and thinking, according to the publisher. The development team studied state curricula, national standards, and teaching methods to make sure test questions were grade-appropriate, interesting, and relevant. Table 11-1 shows the recommended test levels.

The Stanford9 tests specific subject areas differently according to whether the items are multiple choice or open-ended. The following areas are assessed with multiple-choice items:

- Reading
- Mathematics
- Language
- Spelling
- Study Skills
- Listening
- Science
- Social Science

The test assesses the following areas with open-ended (essay or short answer) items:

- Reading
- Mathematics
- Language (through the Stanford Writing Assessment Program, Third Edition)
- Science
- Social Science

Table 11-1   Recommended Stanford9 Test Levels

Grade	Fall Administration	Spring Administration
Kindergarten	SESAT 1	SESAT 2
1	SESAT 2	Primary 1
2	Primary 1	Primary 2
3	Primary 2	Primary 3
4	Primary 3	Intermediate 1
5	Intermediate 1	Intermediate 2
6	Intermediate 2	Intermediate 3
7	Intermediate 3	Advanced 1
8	Advanced 1	Advanced 2
9	Advanced 2 or Task 1	Advanced 2 or Task 1
10	Task 2	Task 2
11	Task 3	Task 3
12	Task 3	Task 3
13	Task 3	

Score Reports

Harcourt Brace offers a wide variety of reports; the most commonly requested reports include basic descriptive data such as percentiles. The development team tried hard to make the reports readable, with colorful supplemental graphs to help parents, teachers, and school administrators quickly understand individual students' and groups' results.

In addition to the common reports such as those presented in Chapter 7, Harcourt Brace provides *lexile measures* that match students' profiles with texts and other instructional materials. There is also a "Thinking Skills" score based on selected items from the different subject areas.

Stanford9 reports feature a "Performance Standards" section developed by teachers that describes what students' results reveal about what the students know and what they are able to do. This report describes students' performance according to criteria for four levels:

- Level 1. Below satisfactory
- Level 2. Partial mastery
- Level 3. Solid academic performance
- Level 4. Superior performance

Related Materials

Harcourt Brace promotes a wide variety of related materials to go along with the Stanford9.

The Guide for Classroom Planning shows teachers how to interpret test results, group students for instruction, evaluate achievement, set instructional profiles, and plan parent-teacher conferences. It defines test scores and types of norms.

For students who speak Spanish, Harcourt Brace offers Spanish-language parallel forms.

The Naglieri Nonverbal Ability Test—Multilevel Form is a language-free measure designed to gauge students' abilities no matter what their educational, cultural, or language background. Harcourt Brace offers this test as an option for ability-achievement comparisons, especially where language-based assessments would provide distorted information.

KeyLinks: The Connection between Instruction & Assessment is a major product Harcourt Brace offers that is designed to help students prepare for standardized tests by providing a series of activities that relate to their daily lives. Students learn effective strategies for obtaining their best scores and become generally familiar with standardized testing.

KeyLinks features new materials in reading/language arts, mathematics, and science. The reading/language arts section provides activities in reading, language, and writing. Reading selections include recreational, expository, and functional passages.

The *KeyLinks* language section includes activities built around real-life scenarios. Focused exercises include activities to help students learn prewriting skills including abilities such as brainstorming and concept mapping, issues of purpose, unity, organization, and language mechanics. In the writing section, students produce extended pieces of writing.

Mathematics activities emphasize real-world content related to common themes. Skills include whole numbers, number sense and numeration, geometry and spatial sense, measurement, statistics and probability, fraction and decimal concepts, patterns and relationships, estimation, and problem-solving strategies. This section also covers process skills including problem solving, reasoning, and mathematical communication.

The science section includes life science, physical science, and earth and space science. Unifying themes of the activities in this section include form and function, constancy and patterns of change, and using evidence and models. The activities in this section emphasize the principles of science.

Strategies for Instruction: A Handbook of Performance Activities, Second Edition, provides grade-specific instructional materials to help teachers gear instruction toward the types of objectives measured by standardized tests and specified by states, school districts, and individual schools. Strategies in this handbook stress connecting instruction across reading, mathematics, language, science, and social science instructional areas.

The Stanford Diagnostic Mathematics Test, Fourth Edition (SDMT 4), provides supplemental information on students' strengths and needs in mathematics. Harcourt Brace points out that if this test is given in the fall, the results can provide additional information to teachers planning appropriate math programs.

Finally, The Stanford Diagnostic Reading Test, Fourth Edition (SDRT 4), diagnoses students' strengths and needs in reading. Just as the SDMT 4 can help teachers prepare math lessons, if this test is administered in the fall, the results can help teachers plan reading activities.

Aptitude Tests

When you get your child's standardized achievement test results, you may see a cryptic score on the report that we didn't discuss in Chapter 3 with a label such as "School Ability Composite" or "Cognitive Ability Index." These refer to scores on group aptitude tests. Many parents don't really understand the difference between achievement and aptitude tests, or between IQ tests and aptitude tests. As a result, they sometimes misinterpret what these scores mean.

To put it simply, aptitude tests *predict* students' ability to learn something in the future. For example, if we want to predict a child's ability to learn calculus, we could give an aptitude test gauging the student's understanding of basic mathematical functions and operations. If we want to predict a child's ability to do well in an advanced writing course, we can give an aptitude test looking at the child's mastery of vocabulary, basic language concepts, and sentence structure and word meanings.

Achievement tests try to *estimate* a student's *current* achievement, and aptitude tests attempt to *predict future* achievement.

Why Give Aptitude Tests?

The main reason schools administer aptitude tests is to gauge their students' readiness to learn new skills. For example, one child may earn his way into Algebra I a year early by his score on the math section of an aptitude test. High school students in particular might face aptitude test score requirements for certain subjects, such as advanced placement courses or courses offered for college credit. In earlier grades, schools give the tests to gauge students' readiness to learn general academic skills.

Unfortunately, some schools use aptitude test scores as the sole indicator of a student's readiness to learn. In fact, in many teacher-parent meetings throughout the nation every year, teachers hand parents these scores and announce that "this is your child's IQ." Many times, students who score above a certain cutoff get into advanced courses, and those who score below do not. The second reason schools give aptitude tests is to compare students' *potential* for learning with their performance. The theory behind this comparison is that a student's actual scores on an achievement test in comparison with predicted levels can be an indicator of the quality of the instruction. After all, if one child with an above-average aptitude for learning in math has below-average scores on math achievement tests, inadequate instruction may be a reason for the discrepancy.

To be fair, other factors that have nothing to do with teaching could also interfere with a student's performance on achievement tests despite estimated potential on aptitude tests. Some of these other factors might include:

- A learning disability
- An uncorrected hearing disorder
- A history of poor school attendance
- Poor educational support at home
- An undetected visual disorder
- An emotional disturbance
- An invalid aptitude or achievement test

If we look at the aptitude-achievement comparisons of a group of students and most students achieve at or above their predicted levels, we would look more closely at students whose achievement scores are significantly lower than their predicted levels. We would want to take a look at those students' actual functioning in school, including grades, homework, and parent and teacher comments, as well as input by the students themselves, to determine whether there is an educational or learning problem.

When large groups of students score much lower on achievement tests than predicted by their aptitude scores, this can be a signal that the school should look more closely at teachers or curriculum. If students who have had Mr. Jones tend to score significantly lower in reading than predicted by their aptitude test scores, perhaps the administration should take a closer look at Mr. Jones' competence or the reading curriculum he uses. If Springfield Elementary uses Program A to teach math and Union Elementary uses Program B, and the students at Springfield score in the predicted range on achievement tests but the students at Union score lower than predicted, perhaps the school should see whether Program B is appropriate. This comparison works in the other direction as well: If students using Program B score much higher than expected while students using Program A score as predicted, perhaps we need to take a closer look at Program B to determine whether we should adopt that program.

Misuses of Aptitude Tests

Aptitude tests are not IQ tests. Individually administered IQ tests examine a student's function in many areas. Although they are controversial, IQ test scores are still used by many educators and psychologists to predict a child's ability to adapt in all areas of their lives that require reasoning. In contrast, aptitude tests examine only a narrow range of skills and abilities that supposedly predict a student's future performance in certain academic skills.

Unfortunately, teachers' and parents' expectations can work both for and against students. Extensive research over several decades has demonstrated that teachers' expectations greatly influence students' learning. In one early study, researchers gave teachers fake aptitude test scores for their students. When they later examined students' grades, they found a strong relationship between the students' fake aptitude test scores and their subsequent grades.

At one time, some schools grouped students according to their scores on these aptitude tests. Although it's now illegal to group by ability based on group aptitude test scores, many teachers, parents, and school administrators still interpret these scores as IQ scores.

So when these scores come home, remember that regardless of how high or low the scores may be, these tests are *not* IQ tests. They are group tests with all the accompanying advantages and disadvantages. Aptitude tests are most useful when used to provide one measure of learning readiness in a very narrow range of skills, especially when applied to groups rather than to individuals.

But you should also be aware that some schools may treat your child differently based on aptitude test scores. If you hear the school personnel refer to the aptitude score as an "IQ score," challenge them. Point out that these tests are only aptitude tests, which assess a much more restricted range of skills than do individually administered IQ tests.

You might also point out that the American Psychological Association, as well as federal law and the test publishers' guidelines, state clearly that individuals should never be diagnosed or classified on a single test . Even when using individually administered tests, psychologists must base diagnoses on what the laws and ethical guidelines refer to as "an array of information."

Test Bias

Test publishers are acutely aware of past problems with test bias, such as when tests used language that was unfamiliar to a student or included tasks to which a student was not exposed. Today, test publishers are very sensitive to possible test bias and go to great lengths to eliminate it.

How to Use Aptitude Scores

When you see your child's aptitude test scores, you should interpret those scores by their percentiles, as we recommended in Chapter 3. Remember that you should only look at an aptitude test score as one bit of information. Although you may be tempted to run through the streets screaming, "My child's a genius!" if the score is high, a very high score doesn't indicate genius. And a very low score doesn't necessarily indicate mental deficiency, either. Unusually high or low aptitude test scores may be a signal for further investigation, but they are inappropriate for diagnosis. Remember that students sometimes just don't do well on tests even though their abilities are fine. If the score on a test is low, look at all the other indicators of how your child is doing and see whether there is a pattern of failure. If you're concerned about your child's score, talk over your concerns with your child's teachers and guidance counselor. An unusually low aptitude test score, or a finding that the achievement test score is significantly lower than the aptitude score predicted, may be an indication that the school psychologist should further evaluate your child's learning.

Aptitude Test Questions

Many times the questions on aptitude tests are similar to those on achievement tests. In trying to predict a student's potential for learning certain skills, sometimes the best way to do that is to find out what skills the student has already learned. The major aptitude tests generally assess some combination of verbal and nonverbal skills.

Verbal Skills

Verbal aptitude tasks estimate a student's ability to reason verbally, which is very strongly related to the ability to master the traditional academic skills that we call the "three R's." Aptitude tests usually measure generally similar thinking skills such as the ability to discover similarities and differences, memory for words or sentences, the ability to define words and follow verbal directions, the ability to classify objects, and the ability to use analogies.

Verbalizing Similarities and Differences.   The following questions might typically appear on an aptitude test:

1 How are an eagle and a hawk alike?

   A They are both marsupials.

   B They are both raptors.

   C They are both crustaceans.

   D They are both bovines.

[Answer: B]

2 What is the difference between a ship and a boat?

   A A ship is bigger than a boat.

   B A boat is bigger than a ship.

   C A ship has a motor, but a boat does not.

   D A boat holds 10 people or less, while a ship holds more than 10 people.

[Answer: A]

Memory for Words or Sentences.   The ability to remember verbal information is important. It's different from the ability to remember nonverbal information, as revealed by the following questions:

[The following questions are given orally.]

1 Write the following words in the same order that I say them: apple; cat; pencil; crispy; wonder.

2 Write the following sentence exactly as I say it: The boy went to the beach, but the water was too cold for him to swim.

The Ability to Define Words.   A strong vocabulary is necessary to learn effectively. Here are two ways an aptitude test may assess vocabulary:

1   Which of the following words means the same thing
    as <u>average</u>?
    A median
    B mode
    C mean
    D standard deviation

[Answer: C]

2   What is a <u>conflagration</u>?
    A a book
    B an argument
    C a meal
    D a fire

[Answer: D]

The Ability to Follow Verbal Directions.   The ability to
understand spoken or written directions is an important verbal skill. Here is a sample of the type of test item that may
assess this ability:

1   Choose the sentence that describes this: "First
    Jason removed his baseball cap, and then he put on
    his cowboy hat."
    A Jason is wearing a baseball cap and holding a
       cowboy hat.
    B Jason is wearing a firefighter's helmet and is
       holding a baseball cap.
    C Jason is wearing an Apache headdress and is
       holding a cowboy hat.

D Jason is wearing a cowboy hat and is holding a baseball cap.

[Answer: D]

The Ability to Verbally Classify.   This ability requires a child to be able to look at material in many ways to detect similar characteristics. For example, an aptitude test may ask the following question:

---

1 Choose the word that goes with the following: oak; maple; sycamore.
   A violet
   B birch
   C oregano
   D strawberry

[Answer: B]

The Ability to Understand Verbal Analogies.   This complex skill requires students to make comparisons, sometimes using highly abstract qualities. For example:

---

1 Bird is to nest as horse is to _____.
   A stable
   B hutch
   C warren
   D den

[Answer: A]

Nonverbal Skills

Nonverbal abilities are much less strongly related to traditional academic subjects such as language arts, but they are strongly related to a student's potential for learning in some other areas, such as graphic arts or technology. Essentially, nonverbal abilities that aptitude tests measure are related to the ability to reason without language. They include several ability areas. The following is just a sample of the nonverbal abilities that aptitude tests may measure.

The Ability to Recognize Sequence.   This skill involves being able to recognize a pattern. For example:

1   Choose the picture that should come next.

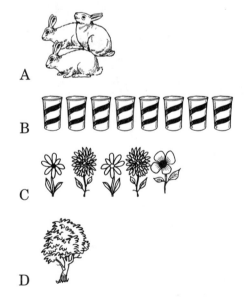

A

B

C

D

[Answer: B]

The Ability to Understand Nonverbal Analogies. This skill is similar to the ability to understand verbal analogies such as the one given earlier in this chapter, but using objects, figures, or other nonverbal examples. This type of question might look like this:

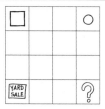

1 Which thing goes into the block with the question mark?

[Answer: A]

The Ability to Discriminate Similarities and Differences in a Picture. This skill requires students to be able to see important aspects of objects and to be able to determine similarities and differences. Possible questions that assess this ability might include:

1 Which picture below is the <u>same</u> as the picture above?

A   B

C   D

[Answer: D]

2 Which picture below does not belong with the others below?

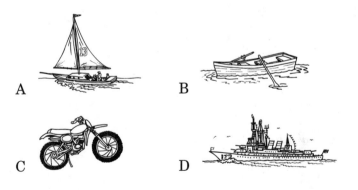

A   B

C   D

[Answer: C]

Quantitative Questions. Quantitative questions simply refer to items that involve calculations and the ability to solve problems using amounts. Aptitude tests try to measure a student's ability to understand the mathematical concepts necessary for more advanced mathematical operations. Here is a sampling of the types of quantitative abilities that aptitude tests may measure.

The Ability to Understand Concepts Related to Quantity. Young children don't understand the concept of quantity. They will sometimes confuse numerical value with size. For example, many young children believe that a nickel is worth more than a dime because the nickel is bigger. As they mature, students will be able to understand more sophisticated quantitative concepts. Consider the following questions:

---

1 Which of these children has the <u>fewest</u> apples?

[Answer: D]

---

2   Which of these is worth the most money?
    A a dollar
    B a dime
    C a nickel
    D a quarter

[Answer: A]

The Ability to Complete Mathematical Operations.
This is one of the skills that aptitude tests may measure
using some of the same questions used by achievement
tests. A student's ability to answer basic math questions is a
very strong predictor of his or her ability to perform more
advanced operations.

The following are examples of the types of test items
that students may encounter:

---

1   $3 \times 5 = $ _____
    A 8
    B 15
    C 2
    D 20

[Answer: B]

2   Angela had $6.00. She paid $1.50 to attend the
    school carnival. How much money did she have left?
    A $7.50
    B $5.50
    C $4.50
    D $10.00

[Answer: C]

3 When Juan visited his grandmother's farm, she had six goats. When he visited her again a month later, the number of goats had doubled. How many goats did she have then?

A 12
B 15
C 3
D 6

[Answer: A]

Group Aptitude Tests

Each major publisher of group standardized tests markets one or more group aptitude tests. As you read about the following aptitude tests, note their similarities and differences. Here are samples of the kinds of aptitude measures that publishers market.

Traditional, Language Based Aptitude Measures

The Otis-Lennon School Abilities Test, Seventh Edition (OLSAT7) is produced by Harcourt Educational Measurement (see also Chapter 11). Students in grades kindergarten through 12 can complete this test individually or in groups in about 60 to 75 minutes. The test assesses abstract thinking and reasoning, which can help school officials understand students' relative strengths and weaknesses in performing a variety of reasoning tasks.

The OLSAT7 reports three major scale scores: verbal, nonverbal, and total. The verbal scale includes verbal comprehension and verbal reasoning. The nonverbal scale consists of pictorial reasoning, figural reasoning, and quantitative reasoning. In this test, quantitative reasoning skills are grouped under the nonverbal area.

The Cognitive Abilities Test (CogAT) from Riverside is another widely used group aptitude test that has been around for more than 40 years. Schools can administer this test in individual or group settings in about 90 minutes. It has levels ranging from kindergarten to twelfth grade.

According to the publisher, the primary purpose of the test is to assess large differences in the ways that students learn. The test reports include scores in four main areas: verbal, nonverbal, quantitative, and composite.

Nonverbal Aptitude Assessment

The Naglieri Nonverbal Ability Test (NNAT) is a test offered by Harcourt Educational Measurement (see also Chapter 11) as an alternative to the traditional, language-based aptitude test. Schools can administer the test instead of or in addition to other aptitude tests in individual or group settings in as little as 30 minutes.

According to the publisher, the NNAT is most useful when students have language problems that could prevent a valid assessment of their learning potential; this includes non-English speakers and those with language-based learning disabilities. The publishers assert that the test is fair regardless of students' educational, cultural, and language backgrounds, and can be used for students with hearing problems or color blindness. The test accomplishes this task by assessing aptitude nonverbally, using shapes and designs not unique to any particular cultural group.

Summary

Aptitude tests try to predict future performance in the class-room or on some other test. They are not IQ tests, although many people mistakenly interpret the scores on such tests this way.

The major test publishers say that group aptitude tests should be used as a way to estimate a student's readiness for instruction as well as to determine whether achievement (as estimated by achievement test scores) is consistent with aptitude (as estimated by these aptitude test scores).

Appendixes

Code of Fair Testing Practices in Education

Prepared by the Joint Committee
on Testing Practices

*T*he *Code of Fair Testing Practices in Education* states the major obligations to test takers of professionals who develop or use educational tests. The *Code* is meant to apply broadly to the use of tests in education (admissions, educational assessment, educational diagnosis, and student placement). The *Code* is not designed to cover employment testing, licensure or certification testing, or other types of testing. Although the *Code* has relevance to many types of educational tests, it is directed primarily at professionally developed tests, such as those sold by commercial test publishers or used in formally administered testing programs. The *Code* is not intended to cover tests made by individual teachers for use in their own classrooms.

The *Code* addresses the roles of test developers and test users separately. Test users are people who select tests, commission test development services, or make decisions on the basis of test scores. Test developers are people who actually construct tests as well as those who set policies for particular testing programs. The roles may, of course, overlap as when a state education agency commissions test development services, sets policies that control the test development process, and makes decisions on the basis of the test scores.

The *Code* presents standards for educational test developers and users in four areas:

A. Developing/Selecting Tests
B. Interpreting Scores
C. Striving for Fairness
D. Informing Test Takers

Organizations, institutions, and individual professionals who endorse the *Code* commit themselves to safeguarding the rights of test takers by following the principles listed. The *Code* is intended to be consistent with the relevant parts of the *Standards for Educational and Psychological Testing* (AERA, APA, NCME, 1985). However, the *Code* differs from the *Standards* in both audience and purpose. The *Code* is meant to be understood by the general public; it is limited to educational tests; and the primary focus is on those issues that affect the proper use of tests. The *Code* is not meant to add new principles over and above those in the *Standards* or to change the meaning of the *Standards*. The goal is rather to represent the spirit of a selected portion of the *Standards* in a way that is meaningful to test takers and/or their parents or guardians. It is the hope of the Joint Committee that the *Code* will also be judged to be consistent with existing codes of conduct and standards of other professional groups who use educational tests.

A. Developing/Selecting Appropriate Tests

Many of the statements in the *Code* refer to the selection of existing tests. However, in customized testing programs test developers are engaged to construct new tests. In those situations, the test development process should be designed to help ensure that the completed tests will be in compliance with the *Code*.

Test developers should provide the information that test users need to select appropriate tests.

Test Developers Should:

1. Define what each test measures and what the test should be used for. Describe the population(s) for which the test is appropriate.
2. Accurately represent the characteristics, usefulness, and limitations of tests for their intended purposes.
3. Explain relevant measurement concepts as necessary for clarity at the level of detail that is appropriate for the intended audience(s).
4. Describe the process of test development. Explain how the content and skills to be tested were selected.
5. Provide evidence that the test meets its intended purpose(s).
6. Provide either representative samples or complete copies of test questions, directions, answer sheets, manuals, and score reports to qualified users.
7. Indicate the nature of the evidence obtained concerning the appropriateness of each test for groups of different racial, ethnic, or linguistic backgrounds who are likely to be tested.

8. Identify and publish any specialized skills needed to administer each test and to interpret scores correctly.

Test users should select tests that meet the purpose for which they are to be used and that are appropriate for the intended test-taking populations.

Test Users Should:
1. First define the purpose for testing and the population to be tested. Then, select a test for that purpose and that population based on a thorough review of the available information.
2. Investigate potentially useful sources of information, in addition to test scores, to corroborate the information provided by tests.
3. Read the materials provided by test developers and avoid using tests for which unclear or incomplete information is provided.
4. Become familiar with how and when the test was developed and tried out.
5. Read independent evaluations of a test and of possible alternative measures. Look for evidence required to support the claims of test developers.
6. Examine specimen sets, disclosed tests or samples of questions, directions, answer sheets, manuals, and score reports before selecting a test.
7. Ascertain whether the test content and norm group(s) or comparison group(s) are appropriate for the intended test takers.

Select and use only those tests for which the skills needed to administer the test and interpret scores correctly are available.

B. Interpreting Scores

Test developers should help users interpret scores correctly.

Test Developers Should:

1. Provide timely and easily understood score reports that describe test performance clearly and accurately. Also, explain the meaning and limitations of reported scores.
2. Describe the population(s) represented by any norms or comparison group(s), the dates the data were gathered, and the process used to select the samples of test takers.
3. Warn users to avoid specific, reasonably anticipated misuses of test scores.
4. Provide information that will help users follow reasonable procedures setting passing scores when it is appropriate to use such scores with the test.
5. Provide information that will help users gather evidence to show that the test is meeting its intended purpose(s).

Test users should interpret scores correctly.

Test Users Should:

1. Obtain information about the scale used for reporting scores, the characteristics of any norms or comparison group(s), and the limitations of the scores.
2. Interpret scores taking into account any major differences between the norms or comparison groups and the actual test takers. Also take into account any differences in test administration practices or familiarity with the specific questions in the test.
3. Avoid using tests for purposes not specifically recommended by the test developer unless evidence is obtained to support the intended use.
4. Explain how any passing scores were set and gather evidence to support the appropriateness of the scores.

5. Obtain evidence to help show that the test is meeting its intended purpose(s).

C. Striving for Fairness

Test developers should strive to make tests that are as fair as possible for test takers of different races, gender, ethnic backgrounds, or handicapping conditions.

Test Developers Should:
1. Review and revise test questions and related materials to avoid potentially insensitive content or language.
2. Investigate the performance of test takers of different races, gender, and ethnic backgrounds when samples of sufficient size are available. Enact procedures that help to ensure that differences in performance are related primarily to the skills under assessment rather than to irrelevant factors.
3. When feasible, make appropriately modified forms of tests or administration procedures available for test takers with handicapping conditions. Warn test users of potential problems in using standard norms with modified tests or administration procedures that result in non-comparable scores.

Test users should select tests that have been developed in ways that attempt to make them as fair as possible for test takers of different races, gender, ethnic backgrounds, or handicapping conditions.

Test Users Should:
1. Evaluate the procedures used by test developers to avoid potentially insensitive content or language.

2. Review the performance of test takers or different races, gender, and ethnic backgrounds when samples of sufficient size are available. Evaluate the extent to which performance differences may have been caused by inappropriate characteristics of the test.
3. When necessary and feasible, use appropriately modified forms of tests or administration procedures for test takers with handicapping conditions. Interpret standard norms with care in the light of the modifications that were made.

D. Informing Test Takers

Under some circumstances, test developers have direct communication with test takers. Under other circumstances, test users communicate directly with test takers. Whichever group communicates directly with test takers should provide the information described below.

Test Developers or Test Users Should:
1. When a test is optional, provide test takers or their parents/guardians with information to help them judge whether the test should be taken, or if an available alternative to the test should be used.
2. Provide test takers the information they need to be familiar with the coverage of the test, the types of question formats, the directions, and appropriate test-taking strategies. Strive to make such information equally available to all test takers.

Under some circumstances, test developers have direct control of tests and test scores. Under other circumstances, test users have such control. Whichever group has direct control of tests and test scores should take the steps described below.

Test Developers or Test Users Should:
1. Provide test takers or their parents/guardians with information about rights test takers may have to obtain copies of tests and completed answer sheets, retake tests, have tests rescored, or cancel scores.
2. Tell test takers or their parents/guardians how long scores will be kept on file and indicate to whom and under what circumstances test scores will or will not be released.
3. Describe the procedures that test takers or their parents/guardians may use to register complaints and have problems resolved.

The Code has been developed by the Joint Committee of Testing Practices, a cooperative effort of several professional organizations, that has as its aim the advancement, in the public interest, of the quality of testing practices. The Joint Committee was initiated by the American Educational Research Association (AERA), the American Psychological Association (APA), and the National Council on Measurement in Education (NCME). In addition to these three groups, the American Association for Counseling and Development/Association for Measurement and Evaluation in Counseling and Development, and the American Speech-Language-Hearing Association are now also sponsors of the Joint Committee.

This document is not copyrighted material. Reproduction and dissemination are encouraged. Please cite this document as follows:

Code of Fair Testing Practices in Education. (1988) Washington, DC: Joint Committee on Testing Practices.

(Mailing Address: Joint Committee on Testing Practices, American Psychological Association, 750 First Street, NE, Washington, DC 20002-4242.)

Note: The membership of the Working Group that developed the Code of Fair Testing Practices in Education and of the Joint Committee on Testing Practices that guided the Working Group was as follows:

Theodore P. Bartell

John R. Bergan

Esther E. Diamond

Richard P. Duran

Lorraine D. Eyde

Raymond D. Fowler

John D. Fremer (Co-Chair, JCTP and Chair, Code Working Group)

Edmund W. Gordon

Jo-Ida C. Hansen

James B. Lingwall

George F. Madaus (Co-Chair, JCTP)

Kevin L. Moreland

Jo-Ellen V. Perez

Robert J. Solomon

John T. Stewart

Carol Kehr Tittle (Co-chair, JCTP)

Nicholas A. Vacc

Michael J. Zieky

APA Staff Liaison: Debra Boltas

APA Staff Liaison: Wayne Camara

Psychometric Statistics Primer

In Chapter 3, you learned some of the important statistical concepts you need to interpret your child's standardized test scores. This appendix will provide a deeper, more comprehensive understanding of the statistics involved in testing.

A Coin-Toss Exercise

In Chapter 3, Figure 3-1 showed a graph of the number of heads that students obtained when they tossed sets of 10 pennies 1000 times. This graph is from an actual exercise the author used with his students. We will use this exercise to present a more in-depth primer of basic psychometric statistics.

The author agreed to teach a course in psychological and educational testing for a small liberal arts college two days before the winter term began. Since this was the first time he had taught the course to students who were not doctoral candidates in psychology, he wanted an idea of how many of the students understood the statistical concepts they would need to complete the course. He administered a pretest and learned that almost none of them knew any of the necessary concepts. He then devised an exercise to help teach them these necessary concepts in a simple way.

There were 25 students in the class. The author went to the bank and obtained $2.50 in pennies, 10 for each student. He had the students push their chairs against the wall and sit on the floor to complete the exercise. He handed out data collection sheets, each of which was marked with the number of possible heads, 0–10. Then the students tossed their 10 pennies and recorded the number of heads. They each repeated this exercise 39 more times in order to produce results of 1000 trials. The instructor collected the tally sheets, entered the individual results into a statistical analysis program, and reported the group's results.

From Table to Graph

Table B-1 shows the number of times that students obtained possible numbers of heads. Using the data from the table, the author was able to make a bar graph, shown in Figure B-1, depicting the number of times each number of heads occurred.

From this graph, we can draw a few tentative conclusions. (Psychologists and statisticians call this practice of drawing a few "quick and dirty" conclusions from the graphical representation of the results "eyeballing.") Just from eyeballing, we can see that there were more scores in the middle of the range than at the two extremes. In fact, the farther we go from the midpoint of the range, the fewer scores we obtained.

Table B-1   Ten Coin-Toss Trials

Number of Heads	Number of Trials
0	0
1	9
2	34
3	100
4	188
5	250
6	227
7	117
8	63
9	10
10	2

Figure B-1   Creating a bar graph from statistics of heads in ten coin-toss trials.

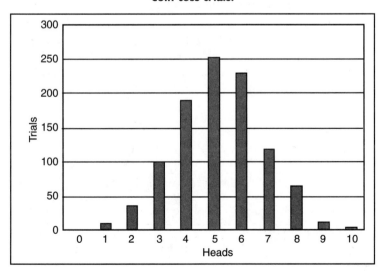

The Normal, or "Bell," Curve

Now let's change the graph a bit. Instead of bars for each number of heads, let's put a dot at the height corresponding to the number of times each number of heads occurred. And let's connect the dots. If we do that, we obtain the line graph shown in Figure B-2.

We see that the curve in Figure B-2 is beginning to take shape. There is a statistical procedure called *smoothing* that smoothes out some of the sharp angles in graphs like this. Don't worry about the exact procedure. Think of it this way: Imagine that the graph in Figure B-2 is made by connecting the dots with fine thread. Now imagine that we connect the dots with a garden hose that won't bend as easily into sharp angles. The resulting curve is shown in Figure B-3. Statisticians call this a *normal curve,* but educators and the media frequently refer to this as a *bell curve* because of its resemblance to the shape of a bell. We obtain bell curves when we look at many traits such as shoe size, IQ, reading scores, number of suicidal thoughts, etc.

Figure B-2   Creating a line graph from statistics of heads in ten coin-toss trials.

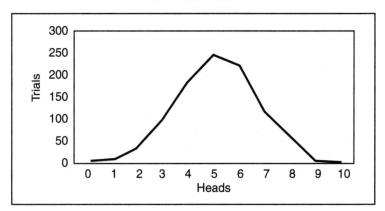

Figure B-3   Smoothing the line graph in Figure B-2 produces a normal, or bell, curve.

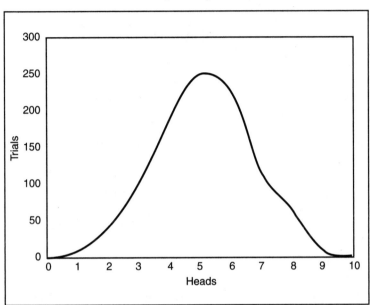

Statisticians have determined some characteristics of the bell curve that are important to us when we test. In fact, most psychological and educational tests are constructed using the bell curve as a model.

Range

The first thing we need to know about scores is the *range*. Since it was only possible to obtain 0 to 10 heads in each trial, we would think that the range of actual scores would be 0–10. Actually, though, if we look at the scores in Table B-1 (at the beginning of this appendix), we see that there were no trials in which there were zero heads. So the range of actual scores is 1–10.

Median

The *median* is the midpoint among scores. That is the point that separates the upper half of the scores from the lower half. We simply rank the scores we obtain from lowest to highest, and the middle score becomes the median. From eyeballing the graph, it appears as if the median is 5, and that is correct.

Mode

The *mode* is the score that occurs most frequently. Again, from looking at the graph, we see that the most frequent score, the mode, is 5.

Mean

The *mean* is simply the average. Theoretically, if the scores make a normal, or bell, curve, the mean, median, and mode should be the same. And sure enough, if we calculate the average number of heads, we obtain 5.174, which is very close. In the normal curve, the mean, or average, is the point of the curve that is in the exact middle, which is what we see in the graph of scores in Figure B-3.

Once we know the range and the mean, we know whether any score is above average, below average, or average. We don't yet know just how much above or below average a score may be, but knowing the mean does begin to help us understand scores. Think of poor Tom who was thrilled when he read that he had made a 92 on the midterm calculus exam. He automatically assumed that the range was 0–100 and that the mean would be quite a bit lower than 92. But when he learned that the range was 0–250 and the average was 165, the 92 did not look so good.

Standard Deviation

Even when we know the range and the mean of the scores, we only know that a score is average, below average, or above average. We don't know how much above or below average a score may be. Suppose that Linda's parents know that she has taken a test with a mean of 500 and has obtained a score of 600. Is that good? We know that it is above the average score, but we cannot say anything more than that until we have more information.

Now we need to know how much the scores vary. That is, for example, are they bunched up near the average, or are they spread out across the range?

We need to know the typical amount by which people's scores deviate from the mean. You might think that all we would have to do would be to record each deviation score—that is, how much each score differs from the mean. If the mean is 500 and Linda's score is 600, then she deviates by +100 points. On the other hand, if Robert's score is 400, he deviates by −100 points. The problem with taking the average of the deviations from the mean is that, theoretically, they should add up to zero! So we need a way to take into account how far the scores are from the mean without regard to whether they are above or below the mean. So statisticians decided to begin by using squared deviations from the mean. (Remember that −7 squared, for example, is 49, as is +7 squared, so squaring the scores solves the problem of the scores adding up to zero.)

We begin by determining each deviation score, squaring it, and adding all the squared deviations. We then divide the sum of the squared deviations by the number of scores we had. In our coin-toss example, that resulted in an average squared deviation of 2.48. But since we are dealing with squared deviations, we must go one step further and take the square root of this number, which, in this case, is approximately 1.58. (We have rounded a lot here, so the numbers are not precise.) We refer to 1.58 as the *standard deviation*.

Once we know the standard deviation, we can understand just how meaningful each score is. For example, we know that if the test that Linda and Robert took has a mean of 500 and a standard deviation of 100, then Linda's score is one standard deviation above the mean, while Robert's is one standard deviation below the mean. Actually, statisticians can construct the normal curve for any group of scores once they know the scores' mean and standard deviation.

Percentiles

Now that we know that the mean number of heads in our coin-toss exercise is 5.174 and the standard deviation is 1.58, we can determine just how unusual each number of heads is. Suppose, for example, that Caroline tosses her 10 pennies and has 3 heads. How unusual is that?

Let's look at Table B-2. This is the same as Table B-1, but with two additional columns. The third and fourth columns are new. In the column labeled "Cumulative Count," we see the number at or below each number of heads. For example, we see that, of the 1000 trials, there were 3 or fewer heads in 143 of the trials. Now look at the fourth column, labeled "Cumulative Percent." The fourth column tells us the percentage of scores at or below that number of heads. That figure is simply the result of dividing the number in the "Cumulative Count" column by the total number of trials (1000) and multiplying the result by 100. Since Caroline is interested in how unusual 3 heads is, she looks at the table and sees that 14.3 percent of the time, students obtained 3 or fewer heads. So 3 heads is a bit unusual.

Table B-2   Ten Coin-Toss Trials Scored

Number of Heads	Number of Trials	Cumulative Count	Cumulative Percent
0	0	0	0
1	9	9	0.9
2	34	43	4.3
3	100	143	14.3
4	188	331	33.1
5	250	581	58.1
6	227	808	80.8
7	117	925	92.5
8	63	988	98.8
9	10	998	99.8
10	2	1000	100

You will see scores on your child's test score report that refer to "percentiles," "cumulative percentiles," "national percentiles," or some other term with the word *percentile* in it. Interpret those scores the same as we do the numbers in the fourth column. A percentile of 43, for example, means that 43 percent of individuals are expected to make scores equal to or lower than a particular score. Chapter 3 gives a table (Table 3-1) for interpreting percentiles. The advantage of using percentiles is that we can compare scores on different tests, even if they have different means and standard deviations, as long as we know the percentiles.

Reliability and Validity

We are not quite finished with statistics just yet. There are two additional concepts that you need to consider when you interpret your child's scores: the test's *reliability* and *validity*. But before we can explain these two concepts in detail, you need to know something about correlation.

Correlation is a statistical procedure that determines how a value of one thing corresponds to a value of another thing. For example, there is a relationship between one's height and weight, another between the speed at which one drives and the miles per gallon expended, and yet another between the number of hours students study and their final grades.

Let's look at the fictitious example shown in Figure B-4, in which a researcher is interested in the relationship between the number of hours that students watch educational television programming and their scores on a reading test. Of course, this is a made-up example: We rarely find such perfect relationships in the real world. But it helps us see what happens when there is a very strong relationship. In this example, the more hours students watched educational TV programming, the higher their scores were on the reading test. When we see that an increase in one thing corresponds to an increase in the other, we say that the two things have a *positive correlation*. A correlation of +1.0 represents a perfect positive correlation.

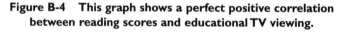

Figure B-4   This graph shows a perfect positive correlation between reading scores and educational TV viewing.

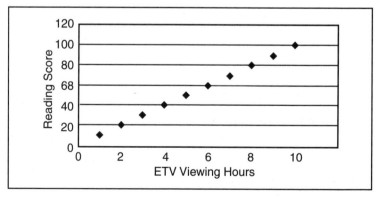

Now let's look at Figure B-5, another fictitious example in which we examine the relationship between the number of hours that students watch prime-time sitcoms and students' reading scores. This time, there is a negative relationship between the two numbers: The more hours that students watch sitcoms, the lower their scores on the reading test. When an increase in one thing corresponds to a decrease in another, we say that the two things have a *negative correlation*. A score of −1.0 represents a perfect negative correlation.

Figure B-5 This graph shows a perfect negative correlation between reading scores and hours viewing sitcoms.

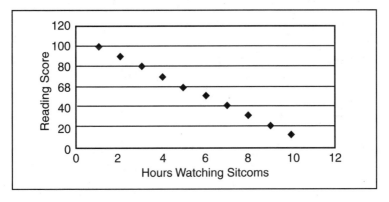

Now let's look at a third fictitious example, shown in Figure B-6. Suppose that researchers are interested in the relationship between the distance students can kick a soccer ball and their scores on the reading test. This time, there does not appear to be any relationship between these two numbers. (In fact, the author made up these data by having Microsoft Excel generate random numbers; a correlation analysis indicated that there is no relationship between them.) When we have two variables in which an increase in one has no effect on the other, we say that there is no (or zero) correlation. We represent this correlation as 0.0.

Figure B-6   This graph shows zero correlation between reading and kicking distance.

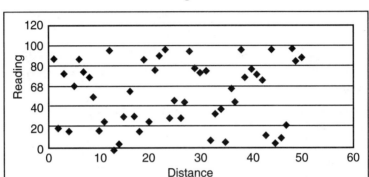

So from these examples, we see that correlations can range from −1.0 (perfect negative correlation) to 0.0 (no correlation) to +1.0 (perfect positive correlation). We won't get into the exact way to calculate these numbers, but these concepts are important in understanding reliability and validity.

Reliability. Reliability refers to the consistency with which we measure something. Suppose that Ross and Kara are laying out a vegetable garden. They know that they have enough seeds for a garden 20 feet wide and 30 feet long. They can measure the distances either by estimating them or by using a tape measure. Of course, they will obtain more consistent measurements using the tape measure than if they simply estimate them, so we say that the tape measure is a more reliable measure of length than estimation.

In testing, we need to know a test's reliability, or the consistency with which it measures whatever it measures. With reliability, we aren't interested in whether, for example, the test is really measuring reading but, instead, whether we can trust that the scores are consistent. In other words, does a child's score one day predict her scores another day?

We express reliability from 0.0 (no reliability) to +1.0 (perfect reliability). In practice, we almost never see perfect reliability. The most technically sound tests typically have reliabilities of 0.9 or above, but it is not uncommon to see tests with much lower reliability.

There are several types of reliability that test manufacturers study, each giving a different estimate of how consistent the scores are. *Split-half reliability* refers to the correlation between scores on one-half of the items of a test and scores on the other half of the items. For example, we might correlate scores on the odd-numbered questions with the scores on the even-numbered items. Or with a test of, say, 100 items, we might correlate the scores on items 1–50 with those on items 51–100.

Test-retest reliability refers to the correlation between a person's scores on two administrations of the test. For example, T. J. might take a reading test today and then again in two weeks. The major problem with test-retest reliability is the *practice effect,* the effect that taking the test previously has on students' scores when the students take the test again. So test-retest reliability tells us how consistent a student's scores are, but only when the students have taken the test at least twice.

Alternate-form reliability tells us how strongly related two or more forms of a test are. You might notice on your child's test score reports that he took a form of the test, such as Form A or Form 2. Test publishers frequently construct more than one form of a test so that students can take the test more than once without having to repeat the same items, that is, without the practice effect. Usually, the forms of a test are very strongly related: Individuals' scores on Form A, for example, strongly predict their scores on Form B.

The *Kuder-Richardson reliability* procedure is a complex statistical procedure for gauging the consistency among scores on test items when students only take one form of a test and take it only once. This procedure is more intricate than the other forms of reliability determination, but the introduction of desktop computers in the 1980s made it much easier for test construction teams to make the necessary analyses using sophisticated statistical software.

Inter-scorer reliability is a particularly important consideration with subjectively scored test items that are increasingly showing up on standardized tests. Anyone who has ever taught a class at any level has had to deal with students challenging their scoring on short-answer and essay questions, term papers, and projects. "You gave me a lower grade because I am (black, white, male, female, left-handed, Democrat, vegetarian)" is known in academic circles as the "student's lament." But it is true that one individual will vary in his scoring and that one individual will score more or less strictly than another. So test publishers are particularly interested in how consistent scores are among different scorers. All test publishers conduct extensive training of those who will score subjectively scored items to try to increase that consistency.

Standard Error of Measurement. From reliability, we can obtain another crucial statistic, the *standard error of measurement* (SE_m). Think of the SE_m as an estimate of the standard deviation of an individual's scores if the individual could take the test multiple times. It simply gives an idea of how reliable any particular score is. When we see scores represented as bands, as we did in the score reports in Chapter 3, those bands were constructed using SE_m. For example, if we wish to express a score in the range in which we would expect it to fall 95 percent of the time, we would express that range as the score plus or minus 1.96 times the SE_m. (For reasons that are beyond the scope of this book, 95 percent of the scores on a normal curve fall between +1.96 and −1.96 standard deviations.)

Factors That Affect Reliability.   Many factors affect a test's reliability. One of the strongest factors that those constructing and norming tests can control is number of scores. All other factors being equal, a test with more items will be more reliable than a test with fewer items. Norming information obtained from a larger number of individuals will be more reliable than that obtained from fewer individuals.

But other factors can affect test reliability. Poorly written test administration instructions, for example, may leave those giving the tests confused regarding what is and is not allowed, which may result in some classrooms following one procedure (such as allowing calculators) and others following another (such as not allowing them). Cheaply produced test booklets may have such faint print that students confuse answers because they cannot read test questions. Failure to specify how much of each test may be administered in one sitting may result in one school's administering the entire test in one sitting and another's breaking the testing up into multiple sessions.

Validity.   In contrast to reliability, which tells us how *consistently* we measure something, validity tells us how *accurately* we measure what we are trying to measure. For example, if we have a test of math calculation skills, are we actually measuring math calculation skills, or are we measuring something else? A math test with a difficult reading level may result in scores that are more closely related to students' reading levels than their math abilities. Or perhaps a school district places students into reading classes on the basis of their scores on a reading test that does not really differentiate students at different levels of reading ability.

Note that a test can be very reliable without being at all valid, but it cannot be valid unless it is also reliable.

We gauge validity several ways. The one way that we can readily quantify is *concurrent validity,* in which we correlate individuals' scores on one test with their scores on another test. For example, if we develop a new test of spelling, we would give individuals our new test and also give them an established spelling test, such as the spelling subtest from the Wechsler Individual Achievement Test. We express concurrent validity as a score in the same 0.0 to +1.0 range in which we express reliability. It is not unusual for test publishers to obtain concurrent validity estimates between their new test and several other, similar tests.

Content validity is not as easily quantified as concurrent validity. Content validity refers to the degree to which a test includes an adequate representation of the skills the test purports to measure. For example, if we develop a test of mathematics computation skills of middle schoolers, we would expect the test to include content from the array of skills that middle schoolers have usually mastered. We would want to make sure, for example, that we included items that assess the ability to add, subtract, multiply, and divide as well as concepts such as borrowing and carrying, computing results of operations involving one, two, and three digits, and understanding how to compute when faced with different notations. Test publishers form teams of educators and test developers to study the academic skills involved in each skill tested. They typically examine other tests, curriculum goals, and task analyses and will attempt to ensure that test items sample the pertinent skills.

Criterion-related validity refers to the degree to which individuals' scores on a test accurately predict the ability of those individuals to perform the skills the test purports to measure. A reading test, for example, that does not actually predict how well an individual can read has poor criterion-related validity. Criterion-related validity has actually been through the courts. In decades past, individuals applying for jobs or for promotions would often compete by taking tests that employers assumed related to the ability to perform the required duties for the positions but for which they could not demonstrate any relationship. Individuals who were passed over for promotions or who were not hired for jobs on the basis of their test scores began to litigate employers for this practice. The courts based their decisions on a simple question: Does the score on the test actually tell the employer whether the applicant can do the job? If employers could not produce the necessary evidence, they were required to abandon their tests. It is possible to quantify criterion-related validity, although the comparisons between test scores and the criteria are less straightforward than with concurrent forms reliability. With criterion-related validity, we must be able to produce some quantified indication of how people perform the necessary skills. For example, if the test is supposed to measure the individual's ability to speak English as a second language, we might gauge the person's success at ordering a meal at a fast-food restaurant, applying for a driver's license, or carrying on a conversation in English. If a test is supposed to tell a potential employer whether the potential employee has the manual dexterity to assemble radios, then the employer must be able to show that scores on the test actually relate to how well they discriminate between those who can and who cannot learn to assemble radios.

We use the term *construct validity* to refer to the degree to which a test measures a theoretical construct or trait such as intelligence, mechanical comprehension, freedom from distractibility, sustained attention, and the like. That is, we are seeking to determine how the test measures broader, more enduring, and more abstract traits. Constructs do not describe those things that exist in a real sense, such as height, weight, or blood alcohol levels. Rather, they refer to fictions we create to describe highly abstract, theoretical phenomena. Because of the abstract, theoretical nature of the traits we are trying to measure, there is often controversy in how we measure them. For example, when we try to measure intelligence, we must first take a position on what constitutes intelligence. If we use David Wechsler's definition of intelligence, for instance, we will assess the individual's ability to perform a wide range of tasks related to verbal versus nonverbal skills. If we adopt Jean Piaget's theory of intelligence, we will look at the qualitative characteristics of children's reasoning, such as whether the individual understands that the amount of a liquid, for example, remains the same whether we pour it into a tall, slender container or a short, fat container. We often find that there are many competing definitions for the constructs and traits we are trying to measure, and each way we define each determines how we measure it.

Summary

This appendix has discussed the basic statistical concepts involved in psychological and educational testing that we lightly touched on in Chapter 3. It dealt with some crucial statistical concepts related to the normal, or bell, curve, including range, median, mode, mean, percentile, and standard deviation. It used concepts from statistical correlation to introduce the statistical concepts of reliability (or the consistency with which we measure something) and validity (or the extent to which we actually measure what we are purporting to measure).

State Education Department Web Sites

STATE	GENERAL WEB SITE	STATE TESTING WEB SITE
Alabama	http://www.alsde.edu/	http://www.fairtest.org/states/al.htm
Alaska	www.educ.state.ak.us/	http://www.educ.state.ak.us/
Arizona	http://www.ade.state.az.us/	http://www.ade.state.az.us/standards/
Arkansas	http://arkedu.k12.ar.us/	http://www.fairtest.org/states/ar.htm
California	http://goldmine.cde.ca.gov/	http://star.cde.ca.gov/
Colorado	http://www.cde.state.co.us/index_home.htm	http://www.cde.state.co.us/index_assess.htm
Connecticut	http://www.state.ct.us/sde/	http://www.state.ct.us/sde/cmt/index.htm
Delaware	http://www.doe.state.de.us/	http://www.doe.state.de.us/aab/index.htm
District of Columbia	http://www.k12.dc.us/dcps/home.html	http://www.k12.dc.us/dcps/data/data_frame2.html
Florida	http://www.firn.edu/doe/	http://www.firn.edu/doe/sas/sasshome.htm

STATE	GENERAL WEB SITE	STATE TESTING WEB SITE
Georgia	http://www.doe.k12.ga.us/	http://www.doe.k12.ga.us/sla/ret/recotest.html
Hawaii	http://kalama.doe.hawaii.edu/upena/	http://www.fairtest.org/states/hi.htm
Idaho	http://www.sde.state.id.us/Dept/	http://www.sde.state.id.us/instruct/schoolaccount/statetesting.htm
Illinois	http://www.isbe.state.il.us/	http://www.isbe.state.il.us/isat/
Indiana	http://doe.state.in.us/	http://doe.state.in.us/assessment/welcome.html
Iowa	http://www.state.ia.us/educate/index.html	(Tests Chosen Locally)
Kansas	http://www.ksbe.state.ks.us/	http://www.ksbe.state.ks.us/assessment/
Kentucky	http://www.kde.state.ky.us/	http://www.kde.state.ky.us/oaa/
Louisiana	http://www.doe.state.la.us/DOE/asps/home.asp	http://www.doe.state.la.us/DOE/asps/home.asp?I=HISTAKES
Maine	http://janus.state.me.us/education/homepage.htm	http://janus.state.me.us/education/mea/meacompass.htm

STATE	GENERAL WEB SITE	STATE TESTING WEB SITE
Maryland	http://www.msde.state.md.us/	http://msp.msde.state.md.us/
Massachusetts	http://www.doe.mass.edu/	http://www.doe.mass.edu/mcas/
Michigan	http://www.mde.state.mi.us/	http://www.MeritAward.state.mi.us/merit/meap/index.htm
Minnesota	http://www.educ.state.mn.us/	http://fairtest.org/states/mn.htm
Mississippi	http://mdek12.state.ms.us/	http://fairtest.org/states/ms.htm
Missouri	http://services.dese.state.mo.us/	http://fairtest.org/states/mo.htm
Montana	http://www.metnet.state.mt.us/	http://fairtest.org/states/mt.htm
Nebraska	http://www.nde.state.ne.us/	http://www.edneb.org/IPS/AppAccrd/ApprAccrd.html
Nevada	http://www.nde.state.nv.us/	http://www.nsn.k12.nv.us/nvdoe/reports/TerraNova.doc
New Hampshire	http://www.state.nh.us/doe/	http://www.state.nh.us/doe/Assessment/assessme(NHEIAP).htm

216

STATE	GENERAL WEB SITE	STATE TESTING WEB SITE
New Jersey	http://www.state.nj.us/education/	http://www.state.nj.us/njded/stass/index.html
New Mexico	http://sde.state.nm.us/	http://sde.state.nm.us/press/august30a.html
New York	http://www.nysed.gov/	http://www.emsc.nysed.gov/ciai/assess.html
North Carolina	http://www.dpi.state.nc.us/	http://www.dpi.state.nc.us/accountability/reporting/index.html
North Dakota	http://www.dpi.state.nd.us/dpi/index.htm	http://www.dpi.state.nd.us/dpi/reports/assess/assess.htm
Ohio	http://www.ode.state.oh.us/	http://www.ode.state.oh.us/ca/
Oklahoma	http://sde.state.ok.us/	http://sde.state.ok.us/acrob/testpack.pdf
Oregon	http://www.ode.state.or.us//	http://www.ode.state.or.us//asmt/index.htm
Pennsylvania	http://www.pde.psu.edu/	http://www.fairtest.org/states/pa.htm
Rhode Island	http://www.ridoe.net/	http://www.ridoe.net/standards/default.htm

217

STATE	GENERAL WEB SITE	STATE TESTING WEB SITE
South Carolina	http://www.state.sc.us/sde/	http://www.state.sc.us/sde/reports/terranov.htm
South Dakota	http://www.state.sd.us/state/executive/deca/	http://www.state.sd.us/state/executive/deca/TA/McRelReport/McRelReports.htm
Tennessee	http://www.state.tn.us/education/	http://www.state.tn.us/education/tsintro.htm
Texas	http://www.tea.state.tx.us/	http://www.tea.state.tx.us/student.assessment/
Utah	http://www.usoe.k12.ut.us/	http://www.usoe.k12.ut.us/eval/usoeeval.htm
Vermont	http://www.state.vt.us/educ/	http://www.fairtest.org/states/vt.htm
Virginia	http://www.pen.k12.va.us/Anthology/VDOE/	http://www.pen.k12.va.us/VDOE/Assessment/home.shtml
Washington	http://www.k12.wa.us/	http://www.k12.wa.us/assessment/
West Virginia	http://wvde.state.wv.us/	http://wvde.state.wv.us/
Wisconsin	http://www.dpi.state.wi.us/	http://www.dpi.state.wi.us/dpi/dltcl/eis/achfacts.html
Wyoming	http://www.k12.wy.us/wdehome.html	http://www.asme.com/wycas/index.htm

Web Sites and Resources for More Information

Homework

Homework Central
http://www.HomeworkCentral.com
Terrific site for students, parents, and teachers, filled with
information, projects, and more.

Win the Homework Wars
(Sylvan Learning Centers)
http://www.educate.com/online/qa_peters.html

Reading and Grammar Help

Born to Read: How to Raise a Reader
http://www.ala.org/alsc/raise_a_reader.html

Guide to Grammar and Writing
http://webster.commnet.edu/hp/pages/darling/
grammar.htm
Help with "plague words and phrases," grammar FAQs,
sentence parts, punctuation, rules for common usage.

Internet Public Library: Reading Zone
http://www.ipl.org/cgi-bin/youth/youth.out

Keeping Kids Reading and Writing
http://www.tiac.net/users/maryl/

U.S. Dept. of Education: Helping Your Child Learn to Read
http://www.ed.gov/pubs/parents/Reading/index.html

Math Help

Center for Advancement of Learning
http://www.muskingum.edu/%7Ecal/database/
Math2.html
Substitution and memory strategies for math.

Center for Advancement of Learning
http://www.muskingum.edu/%7Ecal/database/
Math1.html
General tips and suggestions.

Math.com
http://www.math.com
The world of math online.

Math.com
http://www.math.com/student/testprep.html
Get ready for standardized tests.

Math.com: Homework Help in Math
http://www.math.com/students/homework.html

Math.com: Math for Homeschoolers
http://www.math.com/parents/homeschool.html

The Math Forum: Problems and Puzzles
http://forum.swarthmore.edu/library/resource_
types/problems_puzzles
Lots of fun math puzzles and problems for grades K–12.

The Math Forum: Math Tips and Tricks
http://forum.swarthmore.edu/k12/mathtips/
mathtips.html

Tips on Testing

Standardized Tests
http://arc.missouri.edu/k12/
K through 12 assessment—tools and know-how.

Parents: Testing in Schools

Code of Fair Testing Practices in Education
http:www.hbem.com/home/fairtest.htm

KidSource: Talking to Your Child's Teacher about Standardized Tests
http://www.kidsource.com/kidsource/content2/
talking.assessment.k12.4.html

National Center for Fair and Open Testing, Inc. (FairTest)
342 Broadway
Cambridge, MA 02139
(617) 864-4810
http://www.fairtest.org

National Parent Information Network
http://npin.org

Overview of States Assessment Programs
http://ericae.net/faqs/

Parent Soup Education Central: Standardized Tests
http://www.parentsoup.com/edcentral/testing

The Rights and Responsibilities of Test-Takers
http://www.ipmaac.org/files/ttr0997.htm

General Information on Testing

Academic Center for Excellence
http://www.acekids.com

American Association for Higher Education Assessment
http://www.aahe.org/assessment/web.htm

American Federation of Teachers
555 New Jersey Avenue, NW
Washington, DC 20011

Association of Test Publishers Member Products and Services
http://www.testpublishers.org/memserv.htm

Education Week on the Web
http://www.edweek.org

ERIC Clearinghouse on Assessment and Evaluation
The Catholic University of America
210 O'Boyle Hall
Washington, DC 20064
(202) 319-5120
e-mail: emic_ae@cua.edu
http://ericae.net/.faqs/

FairTest: The National Center for Fair & Open Testing
http://fairtest.org/facts/ntfact.htm

National Congress of Parents and Teachers
700 North Rush Street
Chicago, Illinois 60611

National Education Association
1201 16th Street, NW
Washington, DC 20036

U.S. Department of Education
http://www.ed.gov/

Test Publishers Online

ACT: Information for Life's Transitions
http://www.act.org

American Guidance Service, Inc.
http://www.agsnet.com

Ballard & Tighe Publishers
http://www.ballard-tighe.com

Consulting Psychologists Press
http://www.cpp-db.com

CTB McGraw-Hill
http://www.ctb.com

Educational Records Bureau
http://www.erb-test.com

Educational Testing Service
http://www.ets.org

General Educational Development (GED) Testing Service
http://www.acenet.edu/programs/CALEC/Out_Info_Pubs/GED_facts.html

Harcourt Brace Educational Measurement
http://www.hbem.com

Piney Mountain Press—A Cyber-Center for Career and Applied Learning
http://www.pineymountain.com

ProEd Publishing
http://www.proedinc.com

Riverside Publishing Company
http://www.hmco.com/hmco/riverside

Stoelting Co.
http://www.stoeltingco.com

Sylvan Learning Systems, Inc.
http://www.educate.com

Touchstone Applied Science Associates, Inc. (TASA)
http://www.tasa.com

Tests Online

(*Note:* We don't endorse tests; some may not have technical documentation. Evaluate the quality of these testing programs before making any decisions based on their use.)

Edutest, Inc.
http://www.edutest.com
Edutest is an Internet-accessible testing service that offers criterion-referenced tests for elementary school students, based upon the standards for K–12 learning and

achievement of the states of Virginia, California, and Florida.

Virtual Knowledge

http://www.virtent.com

This commercial service, which enjoys a formal partnership with Sylvan Learning Systems, offers a line of skills assessments for preschool through grade 9 for use in the classroom or the home. For its free online sample tests, see its Virtual Test Center (http://www.virtent.com/testbottom.htm).

APPENDIX

Read More about It

Academic Preparation

Leonhardt, Mary. *99 Ways to Get Kids to Love Reading and 100 Books They'll Love.* New York: Crown, 1997.

———. *Parents Who Love Reading, Kids Who Don't: How It Happens and What You Can Do about It.* New York: Crown, 1995.

McGrath, Barbara B. *The Baseball Counting Book.* Watertown, MA: Charlesbridge, 1999.

———. *More M&M's Brand Chocolate Candies Math.* Watertown, MA: Charlesbridge, 1998.

Mokros, Janice R. *Beyond Facts & Flashcards: Exploring Math with Your Kids.* Portsmouth, NH: Heinemann, 1996.

Schwartz, Eugene M. *How to Double Your Child's Grades in School: Build Brilliance and Leadership into Your Child—From Kindergarten to College—in Just 5 Minutes a Day.* New York: Barnes & Noble, 1999.

Tobia, Sheila. *Overcoming Math Anxiety.* New York: W. W. Norton & Company, 1995.

Turafello, Ann Hunt. *Up Your Grades: Proven Strategies for Academic Success.* Lincolnwood, IL: VGM Career Horizons, 1996.

Vorderman, Carol. *How Math Works.* Pleasantville, NY: Reader's Digest Association, 1996.

Zahler, Kathy A. *50 Simple Things You Can Do to Raise a Child Who Loves to Read.* New York: IDG Books, 1997.

Testing

Abbamont, Gary W. *Test Smart: Ready-to-Use Test-Taking Strategies and Activities for Grades 5–12.* Upper Saddle River, NJ: Prentice Hall Direct, 1997.

Cookson, Peter W., and Joshua Halberstam. *A Parent's Guide to Standardized Tests in School: How to Improve Your Child's Chances for Success.* New York: Learning Express, 1998.

Frank, Steven, and Steven Frank. *Test-Taking Secrets: Study Better, Test Smarter, and Get Great Grades (The Backpack Study Series).* Holbrook, MA: Adams Media Corporation, 1998.

Gilbert, Sara Dulaney. *How to Do Your Best on Tests: A Survival Guide.* New York: Beech Tree Books, 1998.

Gruber, Gary. *Dr. Gary Gruber's Essential Guide to Test-Taking for Kids, Grades 3–5.* New York:William Morrow & Co., 1997.

———. *Gary Gruber's Essential Guide to Test-Taking for Kids, Grades 6, 7, 8, 9.* New York: William Morrow & Co., 1997.

Harris, Joseph. *Get Ready! for Standardized Tests: Grade 1* (Get Ready! for Standardized Tests Series, series editor Carol A.Turkington). New York: McGraw-Hill, 2000.

———. *Get Ready! for Standardized Tests: Grade 2* (Get Ready! for Standardized Tests Series, series editor Carol A.Turkington). New York: McGraw-Hill, 2000.

———. *Get Ready! for Standardized Tests: Grade 4* (Get Ready! for Standardized Tests Series, series editor Carol A.Turkington). New York: McGraw-Hill, 2000.

Mersky, Karen. *Get Ready! for Standardized Tests: Grade 3* (Get Ready! for Standardized Tests Series, series editor Carol A.Turkington). New York: McGraw-Hill, 2000.

Romain, Trevor, and Elizabeth Verdick. *True or False? Tests Stink!* Minneapolis: Free Spirit Publishing Co., 1999.

Talbot, Leslie E. *Get Ready! for Standardized Tests: Grade 5* (Get Ready! for Standardized Tests Series, series editor Carol A.Turkington). New York: McGraw-Hill, 2000.

Taylor, Kathe, and Sherry Walton. *Children of the Center: A Workshop Approach to Standardized Test Preparation, K–8.* Portsmouth, NH: Heinemann, 1998.

Vickery, Shirley. *Get Ready! for Standardized Tests: Grade 6* (Get Ready! for Standardized Tests Series, series editor Carol A.Turkington). New York: McGraw-Hill, 2000.

Glossary

Achievement test   A type of test that measures what a student has already learned.

Age equivalent   A level of performance on a test that represents the average age at which individuals achieve that level of performance. Age equivalents can provide misleading information and should be interpreted with extreme caution.

Alternate forms   Two or more versions of the same test. Test publishers sometimes offer more than one version of a test so they can assess the same skills more than once without repeating the same test. This can be valuable if a student was unable to complete the first test, for example.

Aptitude   Potential for learning a specific skill.

Aptitude test   An assessment designed to measure a child's potential for learning one or more skills.

Battery   A group of two or more educational or psychological tests.

Cognitive assessment   The process of gathering and interpreting information about an individual's ability to perform mental activities related to the ability to learn and interpret information.

Composite Score   A testing score that combines two or more scores.

Confidence Interval The range in which a student's standardized test score might vary if the test is taken again. For example, suppose a child's score is 25 and the confidence interval represented on the report is 20–30. If the child takes the test again, the score the next time would likely be in the 20–30 range.

Content validity   The extent to which a test accurately represents the content it is designed to cover.

Correlation   A way of expressing the relationship between two things, such as score on an achievement test versus report card average.

Criterion-referenced test   A test that compares a student's performance against some criterion. For example, a criterion-referenced test of the alphabet might require the child to recite all letters of the alphabet in order and to write all letters in the correct order in both uppercase and lowercase.

Diagnostic test   A test used to analyze an individual's strengths and weaknesses on some skill. For example, a diagnostic mathematics test would assess students' abilities to recognize numerals 0–9, count to 100, add without carrying, subtract without borrowing, and so on.

Distribution   A tabulation of all possible scores on a test showing each score's frequency.

Frequency distribution   An ordered tabulation of individual scores or groups of scores that shows how many people obtained each score.

Grade equivalent   A score that expresses the estimated grade level that a student's performance on a test represents. For example, if a child's grade equivalent in reading comprehension is 6:2, her reading comprehension is at the reading level of the average student in the 2nd month of the 6th grade.

Group test   A test that a single test administrator can give to more than one person at a time.

Holistic scoring   Subjective scoring of answers to test questions, based on the judgment of the person performing the scoring using specific criteria. This is the type of scoring employed with constructed item responses, such as with short-answer and essay questions.

Individual test   A test that can be given to only one person at a time.

Intelligence   General potential, not a sum of what someone has learned.

Intelligence quotient   A student's score on an intelligence test.

Intelligence test   A test designed to assess a wide array of thinking and reasoning skills related to the ability to adapt and learn. Intelligence tests assess a much wider range of abilities than do aptitude tests.

Mean   Average score of a group of scores.

Median   The middle score in a group of scores ranked from smallest to largest.

Mode   The most frequent score in a group of scores.

National percentile   Percentile score derived from nation-wide norms.

Norm-referenced tests   Tests in which students' scores are compared with the scores of individuals in a test group (called the norm group). With norm-referenced tests, it is the score that matters, not the specific skills mastered.

Normative sample   A comparison group of individuals who have taken a test under standard conditions.

Percentile   The percentage of a group of scores that falls below a given score.

Raw score   A student's actual score before it is transformed into a percentile. For example, if a student answers 27 questions correctly and that corresponds to the 39th percentile, 27 is the raw score.

Reliability   The consistency with which a test measures a trait or characteristic.

Scale   An organized set of measurements, all of which measure one trait or characteristic.

Standard deviation   A statistical measure used to describe the extent to which scores vary in a group of scores.

Standard error of measurement   A statistical measure used to describe the extent to which an individual's scores may vary. The standard error of measurement is expressed as the individual's estimated standard deviation of test scores if he were able to take the test a theoretically infinite number of times.

Standardization The process of developing procedures for administering, scoring, and interpreting the results of tests. As part of the standardization process, test developers will administer a test to a large sample of individuals. Through this process, they determine the statistical properties of the test scores.

Test anxiety Anxiety that occurs in test-taking situations. Test anxiety can seriously impair a child's ability to achieve accurate scores on a test.

Test-retest reliability An estimation of the amount by which a child's scores would be expected to vary from one test to the next.

Validity The extent to which a test measures the trait or characteristic it is designed to measure.

Index

About the Author

Joseph Harris, Ph.D., is a licensed and certified school psychologist who has done extensive research on standardized tests and has consulted on their construction. He is currently adjunct professor at Converse College and owns a consultative practice of child, adolescent, and school psychology in the South Carolina Upstate. Dr. Harris is the author of three of the books in the *Get Ready! for Standardized Tests* series.